How to Pass
FCE

First Certificate in English

Exam practice in
Writing

PAPER TWO

Jacky Newbrook and Nigel Newbrook

Contents

HOW TO USE THIS BOOK

This book tells you what to expect in the writing paper of the new (1996) Cambridge First Certificate Examination, and helps you develop techniques for writing the best answers possible. The book gives you:

- opportunities to practise techniques which will improve the content and presentation of your writing
- clear sample answers with comments on the key points
- sample answers for you to assess, written by students at First Certificate level
- a marking key to help you to assess the sample answers and your own answers
- trial papers
- model answers for you to compare with your own answers

Each chapter focuses on one specific type of composition, and each follows the same pattern:

- an explanation of the question type and what is expected
- examples and exercises to develop techniques for answering that question
- "exam tips" to help you to improve your work
- questions and sample compositions with *our* comments
- questions and sample compositions for *you* to comment on

There are two complete Trial Papers at the end of the book for you to try, with model answers. These models are not the only possible answers, but they provide a framework to help you with your own compositions. Before looking at them, ***use the marking key*** (which is explained on page 4) to assess your own answer first.

WHO WROTE THE COMPOSITIONS IN THIS BOOK?

You may be interested to know that nearly all the compositions used in this book were written by foreign students, aged approximately from 17 to 23. They were studying at or around First Certificate level at an international language school. (Their names are at the front of the book).

Most of the mistakes in these compositions are commented on or are used in exercises, but some of the very small mistakes have not always been mentioned as they are not very serious.

WHAT WILL I NEED TO WRITE?

The composition paper for First Certificate is made up of two parts. The first part is compulsory, so you *must* answer it, and it is always a letter. You are given a task to perform, and clear notes on what to write about. You are always told who you are writing to, and the required style is always clear. It is often formal, or semi-formal. You should follow all the conventions of letter writing in this section although the question may tell you not to use addresses.

There is help with this section in Chapter 2, and with the conventions of letter writing in Chapter 5.

The second part of the paper contains 4 further questions, of which you must choose only 1. There may be:

- an article
- a letter (always of a different style from the letter in the first section)
- a story
- a report
- an argument (which may be a report or an article)
- a question on a set text

The letter may have a task like the compulsory question, but it will usually be in a different style, such as informal; for example, you may be asked to give information to a friend. You may also have to write more formally – for example, you may be asked to write a letter applying for a job or a course of study. You may not need to write the addresses.

In this book you will find sample compositions at the end of every chapter for you to assess and improve. These compositions should help you to see exactly what the examination is asking for in each question type, and how to achieve the best results.

WHAT HAPPENS IN THE EXAMINATION?

You will be given a question paper, and some sheets of paper on which you can make notes and then write your compositions. Remember that you may **not** take any books or notes with you to your exam desk at the start of the examination, or take any of your composition notes away with you at the end of the examination.

Remember to put the number of the question you are answering clearly in the box at the top of your answer sheet, and at the top of every following page. The examiner must be able to see clearly which question you are answering.

You **must** write your compositions in ink, and may **not** use any white correcting fluid.

PRESENTATION

You need to think carefully about the presentation of your writing. It should be easy to read and set out in clearly-arranged paragraphs. If you need to change any words, cross them out neatly with one line through the middle of the word, e.g. "~~elderly~~ elderly". Your writing should look like **(a)** below, and not like **(b)**!

(a)

*It would be so nice for
to go someplace far away f
the city, from its noise a
contamination, a place wher
wouldn't hear about crimes
violence or any kind of bad*

(b)

*people responsible for the
sensors senses an intrude
transmitter will signal to
signal which is connected t
Also Furthermore the Asy*

TIMING

You will have 90 minutes to complete two compositions. In Part 1, you should allow 4-5 minutes to read the question carefully and make sure you understand what you have to do. In Part 2, you should allow 4-5 minutes to select the question that you want to answer. The remaining 40 minutes for each question could be divided as follows:

5 minutes planning + 30 minutes writing + 5 minutes checking

PLANNING AND CHECKING

It is important to write a plan with short notes *before* you start the composition. This will help you to make sure that you answer the question *fully*. There are exercises or comments on planning or preparation in every chapter of this book.

The checking stage is also very important, as you may be able to notice and correct "silly" mistakes before the examiner does! You should look for:

- spelling, e.g. "different", not "differant"
- verb/subject agreement, e.g. "he doesn't have" not "he don't have"
- use of *this*, *these*, e.g. "These cars are expensive" not "This cars are expensive"
- tenses, e.g. "They drove to London yesterday" not "They drive to London yesterday"
- word order, e.g. "The woman drove her car carefully" not "The woman drove carefully her car"

There is more help on spelling in Chapter 2, and there is help with assessing and improving compositions in every chapter.

NUMBER OF WORDS

You need to write a minimum of 120 words and a maximum of 180 words. There is no need to count all the words. Look at the average number of words in your lines. For example, if you write 10 words per line, you should not write more than 18 lines.

PARAGRAPHING

This is very important, as it makes the composition easier to read and also makes a very good impression on the reader. Your ideas should be grouped together in paragraphs, and you should start a new paragraph when you begin a new topic or introduce a new idea. You should indicate the new paragraph either by leaving a line (**a**) or by indenting (**b**).

(a) *Hobbies are an enjoyable way of spending your free time, and there are many different ones to choose from. Many people enjoy hobbies such as stamp collecting. Some people like music, and others like sport.*

My favourite hobby is reading, and I enjoy many kinds of books. I always try to read books that have been made into films, and then see the film afterwards.

(b) *Hobbies are an enjoyable way of spending your free time, and there are many different ones to choose from. Many people enjoy hobbies such as stamp collecting. Some people like music, and others like sport.*
    My favourite hobby is reading, and I enjoy many kinds of books. I always try to read books that have been made into films, and then see the film afterwards.

There are exercises or comments on paragraphing and/or the use of connecting words in every chapter.

PUNCTUATION

There are some conventions that you should try to follow with your use of punctuation. Correct punctuation improves the presentation of your work, and helps the reader to understand your meaning, so you should try to get it right.

There is more help on punctuation in Chapter 5.

THE MARKING OF THE COMPOSITION

Each composition will eventually reach a mark out of 20, providing a total of 40 marks for this exam paper. All five exam papers are worth 40 marks each, making a total of 200 marks altogether.

A 5-point scale such as the one below may be used before the final mark is reached.

Band 5	=	Very good pass
Band 4	=	Good pass
Band 3	=	Pass
Band 2	=	Fail
Band 1	=	Poor fail

Note: the examiner may give a mark which places the composition at the top, middle or bottom of the band selected.

HOW TO USE THE MARKING KEY IN THIS BOOK

The marking key opposite includes most of the points the examiner will be looking for. Use this key when you are asked to assess compositions in this book, or when you want to assess your own writing. If you use pencil, you can rub out your markings and use the key again. The marking key is repeated at the end of the book on page 70. You are permitted to photocopy it if you wish.

In the marking key there are 7 statements in every band. When assessing a composition, put a tick (✓) in the column on the right if you think the statement is true.

For each composition, follow these steps:

1 Start at Band 3 (the basic pass level) and see how many statements you think are true.

2 If you think most of them are true, then move up to Band 4 and see if most of the statements there are true. If not, then the composition is in Band 3.

3 If the Band 4 statements are true, them move up to Band 5.
If they are still true at Band 5, then the composition would be in that band.
If the statements are not true, then the composition would be in Band 4.

4 If you did not tick many statements in Band 3, move down to Band 2.
If you can tick most of the statements, then the composition is in Band 2.
If not, it must be in Band 1.

5 You can check this by looking at the Band 1 statements.

6 Sometimes you may want to tick boxes in more than one Band.
In this case, the composition should be placed in the Band with the most ticks.

MARKING KEY

Band 5
The composition: ✓

a answers the question fully, and with some original points	
b uses a wide range of grammatical structures correctly	
c uses a wide range of vocabulary correctly	
d has the ideas clearly organised in paragraphs	
e uses a variety of connecting words	
f is written in exactly the right style for this type of writing	
g has a very positive effect on the reader	

Band 4
The composition:

a answers the question with enough detail	
b uses a good range of grammatical structures, mostly correctly	
c uses a good range of vocabulary, mostly correctly	
d has the ideas organised in paragraphs	
e uses suitable connecting words	
f is in the right style for this type of writing	
g has a positive effect on the reader	

Band 3
The composition:

a answers the question	
b uses a satisfactory range of grammatical structures, with some errors	
c uses a satisfactory range of vocabulary	
d has the ideas basically organised in paragraphs	
e uses simple connecting words	
f is mostly in the right style for this type of writing	
g has a satisfactory effect on the reader	

Band 2
The composition:

a fails to answer the question fully, and/or is not always relevant	
b uses a limited range of grammatical structures, with errors which make communication difficult	
c uses a limited range of vocabulary with errors which make communication difficult	
d does not have the ideas organised in paragraphs	
e uses few connecting words	
f is not in a style which is suitable for this type of writing	
g does not communicate clearly to the reader	

Band 1
The composition:

a leaves out some parts of the question, and/or has a lot of irrelevant points	
b uses a narrow range of grammatical structures, with many errors	
c uses a narrow range of vocabulary, with many errors	
d has no organisation of the ideas	
e uses no connecting words	
f shows no understanding of the style needed for this type of writing	
g has a very negative effect on the reader	

PREPARING TO DO THE EXERCISES IN THIS BOOK

You will need to understand certain words used in the book to indicate what kind of mistake needs correcting.

Six of these words are:

adjective
adverb
noun
preposition
pronoun
verb

Look at the six underlined words in this sentence, and decide which kind of word they are. The first has been done as an example.

1   2   3   4   5   6

The <u>tall</u> <u>man</u> <u>walked</u> <u>slowly</u> <u>up</u> the hill; <u>he</u> was feeling very tired.

1 adjective
2
3
4
5
6

The answers are on page 58.

You will also need to understand the following kinds of mistakes:

1 When the subject of the sentence does not "agree" with the verb, as in this example:
   The girls <u>hasn't</u> arrived yet.
   "The girls" (noun) is plural, and "hasn't" (verb) is singular, and so the subject and the verb do not "agree".

2 A similar mistake is found with "she work" or "he don't", where the writer has forgotten to put the "__s" which is needed when you have "he, she, it" with the Present Simple Tense. It should be "she works" and "he doesn't".

3 Sometimes the mistake involves the use of an incorrect tense, as in
   We <u>go</u> to London yesterday.
   The tense should be the Past Simple, not the Present Simple, because the action was "yesterday"; it should be
   We went to London yesterday.

4 Sometimes there is an unnecessary word, as in:
   He entered <u>in</u> the room.

5 Sometimes the wrong form of the word is used, as in:
   They are getting <u>marry</u> next month.
   It should be "married".

6 Sometimes "a" or "the" are missing, as in:
   Have you seen book I bought yesterday?
   It should be "the book".
   ("a" and "the" are known as "articles")

7 You will also need to know that the *infinitive* form of a verb such as "do" is "to do", and the *gerund* form is "doing".

Look at the following passage, which contains these kinds of mistakes. The type of mistake is indicated by the number 1-7, which refers to the explanation above. Correct the mistakes, and then check your answers with the corrected passage on page 58.

2   1   4

My friend, John, work in a bank. John and his colleague, Michael, has only been at

1   4   5

there for three months, but they is happy in there. John is going to get marry to

1   6

Michael's sister, Lucy, next month. They hasn't bought   new house yet. Last

7   3

Saturday they spent all day look at houses, but can't find one they liked. They might

6   2   2

have to live in   flat John bought last year. John like his flat but Lucy don't!

WORKING THROUGH THIS BOOK

You should start with Chapter 2, as many of the exercises for Part 1 of the Composition Paper are also relevant to the writing required by the composition questions in Part 2.

In Part 2 of the Composition Paper, there will be four different composition questions. You only need to choose **one** of these, but it may take you 4 or 5 minutes to decide which one to choose.

The last question always relates to the books on the "set book list". If you haven't read one of these books, you cannot answer this question, so your choice is limited to one of the other three questions. These questions will usually involve writing a report or an article, a story or a letter (which will be different from the letter in Part 1).

It does not matter which of the Part 2 compositions (Chapters 3-6) you work on first; they can be done in any order. However, in each chapter, you should do all the Practice Exercises first. They will help you to prepare for the composition work at the end of that chapter.

In the examination paper, the Part 1 composition will be given the number 1, and the four questions in Part 2 may be given the numbers 2-5.

In both Part 1 and Part 2 the compositions must be between 120-180 words. When writing a letter in either part, you will probably **not** need to write any addresses.

SUGGESTIONS FOR FURTHER PRACTICE

If you would like further practice in writing compositions after completing the two Trial Papers, go back to each chapter and select a composition title from one of the Exam Exercises. Write the composition without looking at the book again. When you have finished, compare your answer with the compositions and comments in the book.

PRACTICE MAKES PERFECT

This question is compulsory, so you **must** answer it. You have to use information that you have been given to write a letter, usually in semi-formal style. This simplifies the planning of this composition, as you are given the notes to start with. You should then think carefully about putting the points into complete sentences and organising them into paragraphs. To see an example of how this has been done, look at the set of notes in Exam Exercise 1 on page 11, and then read the first sample composition on page 11.

You are often given more than one task to fulfil, e.g. "Ask for information, **and** ask about the cost". You must do both, otherwise your answer might not be acceptable.

SPELLING

You are not allowed to take a dictionary or spell-check into the examination, so you should not rely on these when writing compositions for practice.

You cannot learn how to spell all the words in English, but you can help yourself when you are practising by writing down all the words you make mistakes with in a separate list and learning these.

There are some very basic spellings which can be confused. Sometimes they are words which look similar, but have different meanings. If you mis-spell these words, you can confuse the reader, because the meaning may not be clear.

Here are some examples of words that may cause problems.

there, their, they're
1 There are twenty students in my class.
2 The students looked up the new words in their dictionaries.
3 The men are building a new school; they're working very hard.

here, hear
1 My favourite restaurant is quite near here.
2 Speak louder, please – I can't hear you.

whether, weather
1 I can't decide whether to buy the red dress or the blue one.
2 In England the most unpredictable thing is the weather.

we're, were, where, wear
1 I'm really excited about my family holiday this year; we're all going to Florida.
2 The football supporters were upset about the bad result.
3 I've lost my dictionary; I can't remember where I left it.
4 I'm going out to a party tonight, but I don't know which clothes to wear.

it's, its
1 It's a pity that the team lost the match.
2 The dog ran round the garden looking for its bone.

how, who
1 I don't know how to play chess.
2 The man who lives next door is French.

whose, who's
1 The boy whose father plays football for England lives in my street.
2 I can't see who's playing the saxophone in the band.

whole, hole
1 In court, the witness promised to tell the whole truth.
2 The mouse lived in a hole under the old house.

though/through
1 Though I like tea, I don't drink it very often.
2 I could see my friend through the shop window.

write/right
1 Please write to me when you arrive in New York.
2 Go along this street, turn right, and the bank is opposite the hotel.
3 The students got all the answers right in the test, and didn't make any mistakes.

Choose the best alternatives in the following sentences. The answers are on page 58.

PRACTICE EXERCISE 1

1 We'd better hurry, otherwise *we're/were* going to be late.
2 *There/Their* are some people who find it difficult to study for *there/their* exams.
3 *It's/Its* a good idea to revise vocabulary before the exam.
4 I don't know *who's/whose* car that is outside – I've never seen it before.
5 Each bedroom in the hotel has *it's/its* own shower and toilet.
6 I can't understand *how/who* it happened.
7 Hurry up, the taxi's *hear/here* !
8 I'm not sure *whether/weather* I should tell her the truth.
9 You aren't allowed to *where/wear* jeans to work at the bank.
10 Speak up, I can't *hear/here* you.
11 I think the *write/right* thing to do is to tell the truth.
12 *Though/Through* the test was difficult, the students all passed.
13 The student answered the *whole/hole* exam paper in less than an hour.

Exam tip

Make sure that you are completely familiar with the spelling of all the "wh" question words, as these are often mis-spelt.

who where when
whose what why which

EASILY CONFUSED WORDS

Some words are confused because
• they look similar, but have different grammatical uses
• there is only one word in other languages, and so bilingual dictionaries don't make the difference clear

Here are some examples of easily confused words.

advice/advise (*advice* is a noun; *advise* is a verb)
1 If you take my advice, you'll study hard.
2 I advise you to study hard.

practice/practise (*practice* is a noun; *practise* is a verb) **exercise** (a verb, it is always physical)
1 There is a tennis practice at school every Saturday morning.
2 It is good to practise your grammar to make your English more accurate.
3 If you exercise regularly, you will keep yourself fit.

recipe/receipt
1 I know a wonderful recipe for chocolate cake.
2 The salesman told me to keep the receipt for the television in case it went wrong.

lend/borrow
1 When you go to the library, you borrow books from the librarian.
2 The librarian lends the books to you.

come/go
1 Come to my room; I want to talk to you.
2 Go away; I don't want to see you again.

possibility/opportunity
1 He has the opportunity to go to the USA next year.
2 There is the possibility that the match will be cancelled.

learn/teach
1 Students learn from a teacher.
2 A teacher teaches students.

bring/take
1 Bring that book to me because I need it here.
2 Please take that book away with you when you leave.

PRACTICE EXERCISE 2

Choose the best alternative in the following sentences. The answers are on page 58.

1 I'm trying to improve my English, so I've bought a good book and I'm going to *exercise/practise* every evening.
2 I've found a really good teacher, so I'm *learning / teaching* a lot.
3 When you visit me, could you *bring / take* my dictionary back, please?
4 I can't really *advice / advise* you on the best thing to do, I'm afraid.
5 She has the *possibility / opportunity* to get a better job.
6 When you buy something in a shop, you should always keep the *recipe/receipt*.

FORMAL / INFORMAL LANGUAGE

It is important to keep the same style all through the answer, in both the compositions you have to write in the exam.

There is more help on formal and informal letters in Chapter 5.

PRACTICE EXERCISE 3

Here are some expressions. Match the formal expressions with their informal version. The answers are on page 58.

Formal
a With reference to your letter
b I would appreciate your help
c I would like to confirm the arrangement
d That would seem to be appropriate

Informal
1 That's fine
2 That's absolutely right
3 About your letter
4 I'd be glad of your help

Note: In formal letters, you do not usually use contracted forms (e.g. "I'd" instead of "I would" or "I had"), but these forms are very natural in informal letters.

PRACTICE EXERCISE 4

In the following letter, the underlined sentences are not in an appropriate style. Change them to be more appropriate for the style of the letter. The answers are on page 58.

Dear Mr Brown,
    Thanks for your letter.
    I am interested in buying the goods you mention, but I have one or two queries that I would like you to clarify.
    The price is fine, but the delivery date is inconvenient; I'd be glad of your help on changing this if possible. Secondly, I would prefer payment to be by instalments.
    I am looking forward to hearing from you,
    Best wishes,
    Joseph Crabtree

EXAM EXERCISES

You **must** answer this question.

In your town, there is a British visitor, Susan Brown, staying with some of your friends. She has been doing some research on local customs and festivals in your country. You want to interview her for your college magazine, and have received the following reply from her:

> How exciting to be interviewed! Yes, I'll be free on Wednesday and Friday morning next week. Which is easier for you? Do you like to make an early start?
>
> By the way, which customs and festivals are you particularly interested in? Would you like me to bring anything to show you?
>
> Best wishes,
>
> Susan Brown

Read carefully Susan's reply, and the set of notes which you have made for yourself. Then write a letter to her, setting up the appointment and answering her questions.

> - why choose this country for research?
> - marriage customs
> - winter festivals
> - SB's photos of weddings/festivals
> - arrange for photos of SB?

Write a **letter** of between **120** and **180** words in an appropriate style. Do not write any addresses.

Look at this answer to Exam Exercise 1, which would be placed in Band 5. Read the composition, and then *look at the marking key* to see why it is such a good answer. Find an example from the composition for each statement in the marking key. Then read the comments to see if you were right.

1   Dear Susan,
         Thank you for your letter. I think that I'm free on Wednesday. Would
     coffee time suit you? I'm not good at getting up in the morning!
         In reply to your question, the readers of my magazine would be
5   interested in finding out what you think about marriage customs and winter
     festivals in Argentina. Could you possible bring any materials you have
     (especially photographs, which can be published in the magazine)?
         The readers may also be interested in knowing your reasons for having
     chosen Argentina to do that research.
10   We generally put some photographs of the interviewee next to the
     articles we publish. Would you mind having some photographs taken during
     the interview?
         I think that the interview will be a very interesting opportunity to
     interchange knowledge.
15   I'm looking forward to meeting you soon.
         Yours sincerely,
         Maria Gonzalez

Comments

a all the points are mentioned, with original detail such as *line 3* "I'm not good at getting up in the morning."

b *line 8* "The readers may also be interested in knowing your reasons"

c *line 3* "Would coffee time suit you?"

d each paragraph relates to the format given in Chapter 5 (Letters), although there is an extra paragraph in the ending section

e *line 4* "In reply to your question" is a nice connecting phrase

f/g the style is right, and the effect is very positive

The vocabulary in *line 14* could be expressed more naturally: "interchange knowledge" should be "share our ideas".

line 16 "yours sincerely" is appropriate here, but she could also have used "with best wishes" as the letter is friendly. There are very few connecting words, which is not a problem in this letter as the writer has managed to order and connect the ideas through the sentences themselves. However, it is usually better to use some connecting words in case this control breaks down. For example, she could have used "moreover" or "furthermore" to start *line 8*.

SAMPLE COMPOSITION 2

Here is another sample answer to Exam Exercise 1. *Use the marking key* and try to grade it. Then read the comments to see if you were right.

1   Dear Susan,
         Thank you for your reply. I'm glad that you'll be able to talk to me.
         Well, firstly I'd like to make sure of the date. You'll be free on
      Wednesday and Friday morning, won't you. I'd prefer on Wednesday also I'd
5   like to make an early start because I think it'll take a long time to do the
      interview. How about starting it from 9am? Secondly, I'm interested in
      customs and festivals.
         We're going to interview you why you chose this
      country for research and how you think about marriage customs and winter
10   festivals of our country since you've been doing some research. At that time I
      also need your photos of weddings and festivals. Could you bring some photos
      with you? If you don't mind, I'd like to arrange for photos of you as well.
         Anyway, if you've got a problem, could you tell me about that.
      I'll arrange it for you. Then I'm looking forward to seeing you next
15   Wednesday.
         Best wishes,

Comments

You should have ticked boxes **a**, **d**, **e**, **f**, **g** in Band 4, and boxes **b**, **c** in Band 3.

The writer has answered every part of the question. Some grammatical structures are not correct, such as:

line 8 "to interview you why you chose" should be "to ask you why you have chosen"

line 9 "how you think" should be "what you think"

line 10/11 should be written in the future "At that time I will need"

line 13 the expression is wrong; it should be "If there is a problem, could you let me know?"

The presentation is good, with good indenting and punctuation, although there is a ? missing in *line 4*. There should be a new sentence in *line 4* beginning "I'd like to ..." as this is a new idea.

There is good use of connecting words; the use of "firstly, secondly" is very clear, and "well", and "anyway" are used very naturally.

The style is right for this type of writing.

Now look at this answer, ***use the marking key*** and try to grade it. Then compare it with Sample Composition 2, and see how clearly you can see the differences between the two answers. Then read the comments to see if you were right.

1   Dear Susan Brown,
     I thank you your leter which it come yesterday. I can think you have good time
     here. I want know why do you come my country. Yes I come wensday morning
     and I bring photographs for you. Customs in my country is very nice and in
5   winter also. Chrismas is good time for us this is big festival. I want ask you
     how is Chrismas in your country.
     I hope I see you next week. I suggest 10.00 is good time what is your opinion.
     If you like phone me my number is 48572. My friend don't come with me
     but he give you greetings.
10   Yours faithfully
     John

Comments

You should have ticked all the boxes in Band 1.

The writer has omitted some parts of the question; he has not mentioned marriage at all, and he has misunderstood the question about photographs. The letter is full of basic grammatical errors, and the vocabulary is very limited and occasionally wrong, e.g. *line 9* "give you greetings", which should be "sends his regards". This information is irrelevant.

There are no paragraphs, and the ideas are not presented logically or with any organisation. There are no connecting words, and the letter is very difficult to understand.

There are several spelling mistakes, e.g. "leter" should be "letter". (This is a very bad mistake, as the word is given in the question.)

The letter conventions are not followed – it is not correct to begin a letter with the full name, and the ending should be either "Yours sincerely" or "With best wishes".

All these factors create a very negative effect on the reader.

There is an improved version of this composition in the answers on page 59.

Exam tips

1 Remember that some of the information in the question may be produced in note form, but *you* must write in full sentences. For example, it may say
       "Why choose this hotel?"
   You should write
       "Why did you choose this hotel?"
   or
       "Can you tell me why you chose this hotel?"

2 When you write the composition, tick off the points under the illustration as you mention them in your answer. Then, when you have finished, go back and check that all the points have been ticked, so that you are sure that you have covered everything in your answer.

EXAM EXERCISE 2

You **must** answer this question.

Your family is interested in a holiday in the "Little Princess" houseboat, but only has the advertisement shown below. You need more information. You have the task of writing to "Holiday Cruises", which published the advertisement.

Read carefully the advertisement and the notes which you have made below. Then write your letter to Holiday Cruises, covering the points in your notes and adding any relevant information about your family.

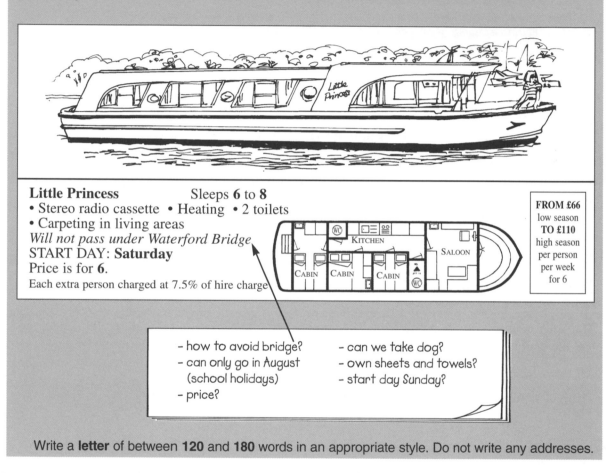

Little Princess   Sleeps **6** to **8**
• Stereo radio cassette • Heating • 2 toilets
• Carpeting in living areas
Will not pass under Waterford Bridge
START DAY: **Saturday**
Price is for **6**.
Each extra person charged at 7.5% of hire charge

FROM £66
low season
TO £110
high season
per person
per week
for 6

- how to avoid bridge?
- can only go in August (school holidays)
- price?
- can we take dog?
- own sheets and towels?
- start day Sunday?

Write a **letter** of between **120** and **180** words in an appropriate style. Do not write any addresses.

SAMPLE COMPOSITION 1

Here is a sample answer to Exam Exercise 2. *Use the marking key* and try to grade it. Then read the comments to see if you were right.

1   Dear Sir/Madam,
        I am writing to enquire for more information about the holiday, which
    was published in the "Holiday Cruises" brochure.
        Unfortunately I can only go in August because the holiday begins on
5   the 31st July. As a result I have to go so late, I will arrive on Sunday. Due to
    the fact that the holiday is in the high season, the price will change from £66 to
    £110 each, which makes the holiday too expensive if you have got four
    children.
        I hope you can arrange a special price for us.
10   By the way, I could not read if I have to take sheets and towels: and my
    last question, it is possible that I can bring my dog.
        Finally, I have not got any details about a route, which I would not pass
    the low bridge at Waterford.
        I look forward to hearing from you and I am grateful for giving
15 information.
        Yours faithfully,

Comments

You should have ticked all of the boxes in Band 3. The writer has answered the question, and the range of grammatical structures and vocabulary is satisfactory.

Although there are errors, they do not make communication difficult. These include:

line 2 "enquire for more information" should be "ask for more information"

line 5 "As a result I have to go so late" should be "Because I cannot go until late"

line 6 "the price will change" should be "the price changes"

line 10 "I could not read if" should be "I could not see whether"

line 11 "it is possible that I can bring my dog" should be "is it possible for me to bring my dog?"

line 12 "which I would not pass" should be "which would avoid"

The paragraphing is basically satisfactory, although line 9 should not start a new paragraph.

Now read this sample answer to the same Exam Exercise, *use the marking key* and try to grade it. Then answer the following questions, which focus on accuracy and on style. You will find comments and answers to the questions on page 59.

SAMPLE
COMPOSITION 2

1   Dear Sir or Madam,

       I'm writing this letter to ask you about the "Little Princess" houseboat. I watched the advertisement for this houseboat yesterday and I'm very interested in it so I need more information about it.

5   First of all, my family consists of four members, my husband, my mother, my daughter (six years old) and I. We also have a dog.

       We can only go in August in the school holidays. Please let me know the price for three adults and one child. I'd like to take our dog if possible as we can't leave him alone in our house. Do you have sheets and towels or do

10   we have to take our own? Is it possible to start on Sunday? It's more convenient for us. Can we do "karaoke" or dance there? What kinds of activity do you have?

       Looking forward to receiving your reply soon.

       Yours faithfully,

Questions

1 Has she forgotten to ask any questions?

2 Is the style formal?

3 Has she given any extra information that is interesting?

4 Find the mistakes in the following lines:

    line 3   wrong verb

    line 13 style unsuitable

**EXAM
EXERCISE 3**

You **must** answer this question.

You are interested in taking a course at a local college, but you have only got the information in this advertisement from the local newspaper. Your friend is already studying at the college, but you haven't seen him for quite a long time.

Read the advertisement and the notes you have made below. Then write a letter to your friend in an appropriate style, covering the points in your notes and telling him which course you are interested in.

REGIONAL COLLEGE

COURSES MAY BE TAKEN IN THE FOLLOWING TOPICS,
SUBJECT TO THE USUAL ENTRY REQUIREMENTS:

**FRENCH • COOKERY • ENGLISH LANGUAGE
TOURISM • COMPUTING**

THE COLLEGE OFFERS A WIDE RANGE OF SOCIAL ACTIVITIES,
AND HAS EXCELLENT FACILITIES FOR BOTH STUDY AND LEISURE.

---

* which social activities – what does this include?
* what facilities are there?
* other students friendly?
* teachers good?
* good library?

Write a **letter** of between **120** and **180** words in an appropriate style. Do not write any addresses.

**SAMPLE
COMPOSITION 1**

Here is a sample answer to Exam Exercise 3. *Use the marking key* and try to grade it. Then read the comments to see if you were right.

1   Dear Marcia,
      I'm writing to ask some information about the Regional College, since
I'm considering taking a course there next term. You must be a bit surprised,
as we haven't been in touch for so long, but I met your mother in town a
5   couple of days ago and she told me you were studying there.
      I've read an advertisement for the college, but I still have some
questions. First of all, I'd like to know which kind of social activities they
offer, and what they include as well.
      I'd also like to know about the facilities the college provide – mainly if
10 there's a laundry. I can't stand going back and forth with dirty clothes bags,
and I've heard the college is quite far from town.
      How about the other students? Is it easy to make friends with them or
are they the kind of people who couldn't care less about "strangers"? By the
way, are the teachers interested in the students' needs? Your mother said they
15 are well-qualified, but I'd like to know your opinion about it just the same.
      Lastly, I wonder if they have up-to-date materials in the library. I
believe you can remember my huge appetite for books!
      I'm looking forward to hearing from you.
      Best wishes,

Comments

You should have ticked all the boxes in Band 5.

This is an excellent answer. It asks all the necessary questions, with original details e.g. *line 10*. The wide range of structures and vocabulary includes:

line 2/3 "since I'm considering taking a course there"

line 9/10 "mainly if there's a laundry"

line 16 "I wonder if they have up-to-date materials in the library"

line 17 "my huge appetite for books"

It is very well presented, with clear paragraphing and indented layout, and the style is exactly right.

This is a very comprehensive answer.

Exam tip

This answer is too long, but the writer has been able to maintain the style and accuracy. However, this extra length could lose you marks if it is irrelevant or inaccurate, and so you should try not to write more than 180 words.

Now read this sample answer to the same Exam Exercise. *Use the marking key* and try to grade it. Then answer the questions, which will focus on presentation and accuracy. You will find comments and answers to the questions on page 59.

SAMPLE COMPOSITION 2

1   Dear Michele,
          I was happy to receive your postcard: it seems that you really like the
     place.
          So, I've finally made up my mind and decided to spend some time at
5   your college.
          In fact, I've seen its advertisement in the local newspaper and I'm
     interested in taking a French course, because I studied it some years ago but,
     not having the chance to practise it, I almost forgot everything.
          However, this is the same course you're attending and I'd like from you
10   some information that I couldn't find in the ad. What does, for example, the
     "wide range of social activities" include? And what "excellent facilities" are
     there? However, these are not the most important things or, at least, not as
     important as the teachers, for instance: are they really good? And what about
     the library?
15   Then, you seem to have a really great time there: it means that the other
     students are friendly, aren't they?
          As soon as I receive this information earlier we could meet there (I haven't
     seen you for ages!)
          Looking forward to hearing from you soon,
     Love,

Questions

1 What do you think about the paragraphing?
2 Could you rewrite *lines 6-8* to make the meaning clearer and correct the tense mistakes?
3 Find the mistakes in the following lines:

line 9/10 word order

line 15 wrong tense

line 17 unnecessary word

In Part 2 of the Composition Paper, you must choose only one composition question. There is usually a question that asks you to write either a report or an article.

This can involve either writing a report for a company, or writing an article for a magazine or newspaper. Both a report and an article can involve presenting two sides of an argument, but they are rather different in style and purpose.

WRITING A REPORT

A report
- is usually written in a formal style
- is usually more factual and detailed than an article
- is normally written for only one person to read, in some sort of business or work situation
- presents facts about an event or a situation so that the reader understands everything clearly
- may contain recommendations
- is not intended to entertain, but to give information
- may have a special layout, as it may also contain headings
- may use set phrases, often using the passive voice, such as "it is recommended that"

CONNECTING IDEAS

For this composition, you may need to present the points on both sides of the question being considered. The style will need to be quite formal, and so you will need to use linking words in your sentences. You could connect the two sides of your argument by introducing them with quite formal connectors such as:

> *On the one hand, ...*
> *On the other hand, ...*

(**Note:** you can just use "On the other hand" to introduce the opposite point, even if you didn't say "On the one hand".)

You will also need to connect your sentences within each main paragraph. If you are making three main points, you could introduce them by saying:

> *Firstly, ...*
> *Secondly, ...*
> *Finally, ...*

If you are introducing the other side of an argument in the second part of your report, you could say:

> *One point is ...*
> *Another point is ...*
> *A final point is ...*

You could also introduce the second or third points by saying:

> *Furthermore, ...*
> *Moreover, ...*
> *In addition to this, ...*

For example:"One problem with this hotel is its great distance from the city centre. Furthermore, the poor bus service makes it difficult to get back after 6 p.m. in the evening."

These are all quite formal, and are not suitable in an article.

Don't forget to use basic "connectors" as well, such as those in italics below (**Note:** you shouldn't use "and" or "but" to start sentences in a report, as these are joining words.)

"I would recommend this hotel because of the friendly staff, *although* the manager is rather strict. *Despite* this, he did try to help us when we lost our luggage, but we still couldn't find it. *However*, this didn't spoil our stay at the wonderful Palace Hotel."

Choose the correct connector. The answers are on page 59.

PRACTICE EXERCISE 1

1 We played tennis *although/despite* it was raining.
2 *Although/Despite* his broken leg, he played football.
3 We stayed three weeks at that hotel *because/although* it was so wonderful.
4 I like seaside holidays *but/however* my wife prefers walking in the mountains.
5 *However/But*, our holiday last year was a great success.

Note: You cannot say "Despite his missed train, he arrived on time." You have to say "Despite the fact that he missed his train, he arrived on time." or "Despite missing (having missed) his train, he arrived on time."

Put the following connecting words or phrases into the passage below. The answers are on page 59.

PRACTICE EXERCISE 2

In addition to this,
However,
Secondly,
Finally,

"As we have seen, the Majestic Hotel has many good points. _____, there are some negative ones concerning the restaurant. Firstly, it is too small for such a large hotel. _____, the chef does not cater for vegetarians. _____, he is reluctant to discuss any kind of personal request with the guests. _____, it is never open early enough for families with young children.

The following four paragraphs from a report on a hotel are in the wrong order. Put them in the correct order. The answer is on page 59.

PRACTICE EXERCISE 3

a On the other hand, however, the disappointments concerning food and nightlife might outweigh the plus points. Firstly, the range of meat on offer is limited to chicken and pork.
b A final point concerns the complete absence of any kind of social activity after 9 o'clock in the evening. Surely there could be some discos or parties occasionally?
c On the one hand, staying at this hotel offers tourists the chance of sampling the high life at a relatively low cost, especially outside the peak season.
d Secondly, there seems to be no provision for vegetarians, and no attempt to provide an early evening meal for young families.

The following notes were made at a meeting of local people about plans for holding a festival in the town. The notes need to be expanded into a report to be given to the chairman of the local committee, recommending the festival. Write the report from the notes, keeping the order as given but adding any words you feel are necessary to make it clear. Use connectors and use paragraphs if necessary. There is a model answer on page 60.

PRACTICE EXERCISE 4

• Festival to take place over 3 days – suggest Fri/Sat/Sun, end July.
• Place – Central Park.
• Visitors' parking behind church.
• Money raised for local charities – suggest cancer research.
• Festival good idea – bring business to town for shops, restaurants and hotels.

PLANNING

This is very important, as you need to write your ideas clearly.

Here is an example of a plan for a report on a new leisure centre in your town.

You could divide your notes like this:

Positive
- excellent swimming pool
- good changing facilities
- sports hall can be used for
  four different sports
- drinks and food available
  in cafeteria

Negative
- limited parking space
- too far from town centre
- no reductions for families
  or retired people
- closed on public holidays

You could then put these points into two main paragraphs, connecting them using the connecting words suggested at the start of the chapter.

EXAM EXERCISES

EXAM EXERCISE 1

Your teacher is doing a survey on which films are most popular at the moment and why. She has asked you to write a **report** on a film you have seen recently which is very popular. Say what happens in the film, what is good about it and why you think it is so popular.

SAMPLE COMPOSITION 1

Here is a sample answer to Exam Exercise 1. *Use the marking key* and try to grade it. Then read the comments under the answer to see if you were right.

1   Film: Dangerous Minds

Length: 120 minutes

Comments:
I won't be able to give you an exact review or report of this movie because
5   everybody watches it from another point of view but let me try to give you a
frame.

The whole film is a drama with a few jokes and a sort of happy end. It plays
in a poor quarter of a metropolis in the States. Michelle Pfeiffer, who act in
the main role, applied for a job as a teacher in a public school. Her class was
10   a difficult class without discipline and friendliness. Most of the students had
no family background and joined a gang. So it was very difficult for Michelle to
teach them. The film shows how she tried at first and how she changed her
way of teaching.

In my opinion it is a very good and interesting film for all ages over 14,
15   especially for teachers. In the story they have a lot of problems (and perhaps
solutions) which today's teachers have to fight with. Also for students it could
be interesting because they can see the point of view of a teacher.
Anyway, if you haven't seen it already, go and watch it! It may broaden your
mind!

Comments

You should have ticked boxes **a**, **c**, **d**, **e**, **g** in Band 4, and boxes **b**, **f** in Band 3.

The description of the film is clear and easy to follow, and it answers all parts of the question, although there could have been more details on why the film is popular.

There are some grammatical mistakes:

line 7   "plays" should be "takes place"

line 8   "act in" should be "has"

line 16 "Also for students it could be interesting" is wrong word order, and should be "It could also be interesting for students"

Some vocabulary is inaccurate:

line 5   "everybody watches it" should be "everybody sees it"

line 6   "frame" should be "general idea".

There is a very good expression in *line 18*: "it may broaden your mind".

The answer is well-expressed and well-organised, with a practical layout which is clear and suitable. The style is mostly right for this type of writing, although the final sentence is a bit too informal for a report.

Now read this sample answer to the same Exam Exercise, *use the marking key* and try to grade it. Then answer the questions, which will focus on accuracy and organisation. You will find comments and answers to the questions on page 60.

SAMPLE COMPOSITION 2

1   What could happen if a progressive English teacher would arrive in a
      traditional school in USA?
      What could happen to the students if a rational and serious way of teaching
      would be changed with the feelings and heart's way?

5   That is what happens in "Dead Poet's Society", a movie by Peter Weir.
      A fantastic Robin Williams plays the role of the revolutionary teacher
      John Keating who tries to inspire his students to follow their passions and emotions.
      The class will love him, but not everything will be good. Sometimes impulses
      can be dangerous and some events can be misinterpreted.

10   The movie's message is directed towards heart and can't miss: you
      mustn't be oppressive, just rational and close, because if you do it the damage
      is to break lives, to destroy feelings, to throw people into love for foolish and
      senseless.
      I think that the message is the reason because of which the movie has become

15   so popular: listen to your heart; it is the best way to feeling and living life.

Questions

1 Find the mistakes in the following lines:

lines 1-4 two conditional sentences

line 10 missing article

2 How could you improve the presentation?

EXAM EXERCISE 2

You have recently started work for a company that publishes a guide to restaurants. You have visited the "Old Farmhouse" restaurant, and must now write your report for your boss.

Write your **report**, describing the restaurant, what it has to offer tourists and commenting on its good and bad points.

Here is a sample answer to Exam Exercise 2. *Use the marking key* and try to grade it. Then read the comments under the answer to see if you were right.

SAMPLE COMPOSITION 1

1   The "Old Farmhouse", a nice old restaurant in cottage style, is situated in the
      hilly countryside outside of Stratford-upon-Avon. It is quite easy to reach it by
      car because it isn't far away from the road no.A1507 and it is well signed.

      In its area it is famous for its nice atmosphere, the friendly service and the

5   excellent food. The food is really marvelous. They are specialised in game and
      offer a big choice of different meats, vegetables, drinks, wines, desserts ...
      It takes almost more time to choose the right meal than to eat it. Then, there

are also meals for children available or you can order a half portion without any problems.

10 Finally, what about the money? The prices aren't low but when you look what you get for your money, they are OK.

So, when will you be there? Today or tomorrow evening? Anyway, don't forget to place a reservation!

Comments

You should have ticked boxes **b**, **d**, **e**, **g** in Band 4 and boxes **a**, **c**, **f** in Band 3.

There is a good range of grammatical structures, with some minor mistakes:

line 2 "It is quite easy to reach it by car" should be "it is quite easy to reach by car"

line 5 "They are specialised in game" should be "They specialise in game"

The vocabulary is sometimes inaccurate:

line 3 "the road No. A1507" should be "the A1507"; "it is well-signed" should be "it is well sign-posted".

The paragraphing is good, with good connecting words.

The report begins in an appropriate style but this is not maintained; the last paragraph is too informal, and is more suitable for an article; in a report it should be: "I recommend this restaurant to both families and business people for excellent meals at fairly reasonable prices".

The use of OK is also inappropriate, and the exclamation marks are too informal.

SAMPLE COMPOSITION 2

Now read this sample answer to the same Exam Exercise, *use the marking key* and try to grade it. Then answer the questions under the answer, which will focus on accuracy. You will find comments and answers to the questions on page 60.

1 The "Old Farmhouse" it's very nice and beautiful situated in a small town about fifteen minutes from the city.

The location is marvellous, being in countryside, and the restaurant itself it's perfect for a couple of lovers. It is decorated in an old style, intimate
5 atmosphere, candles on the tables and you can have a good meal there for £20 and the bar it's quite good too.

But there are three bad points in this restaurant. Firstly, is situated in a very beautiful small town where you can only reach by car and it's also a bit difficult to find.

10 Another thing is that the fish is not so good so I suggest to eat a fabulous beefsteak. Finally, and in my own opinion the most important point, it's that the waitress are not very kind or nice, and this could break the romantic and relaxing atmosphere that have the restaurant.

Anyway, I suggest going there and trying it.

Questions

Find and correct the following mistakes:

line 1 unnecessary pronoun / adverb form needed
line 3 unnecessary pronoun
line 4 preposition missing
line 6 unnecessary pronoun
line 7 wrong connector / pronoun missing
line 8 wrong "wh" word
line 10 gerund needed
line 11 unnecessary pronoun
line 13 word order / agreement between subject and verb

WRITING AN ARTICLE

An article
- is a piece of writing usually for a newspaper or magazine
- is written in an interesting and entertaining way
- gives opinions and ideas as well as facts
- is written for many people to read, so you need to keep their attention
- may include some funny stories, colourful descriptions or reported speech
- is in a less formal style than a report

The sentences in the following article about a train crash are mixed up. Put them in the correct order, and then answer the questions at the bottom of the exercise, which will help you to check the order of the sentences. The answers are on page 60.

PRACTICE EXERCISE 5

a Both trains were full, not only with commuters but also shoppers returning home after a day at the sales, and this made the trains unusually busy.

b Ambulances arrived quickly, and took the injured to hospital, although luckily none was badly hurt. However, trains were delayed for several hours.

c Describing this scene, one shopper said, "It was terrible! Everyone was screaming and panicking, and no-one seemed to know what to do."

d Many people were carrying full shopping bags, which were thrown around the carriages, adding to the general confusion.

e There was an accident last night on a railway line just south of London, when two trains collided on a busy commuter line at six o'clock yesterday evening.

f A spokesman for the railway company said "We are sorry about this, but we will do our best to get things moving again".

1 What is "this" in (**f**)

2 What is "it" in (**c**)?

Words like "it", "they", "this" always refer to something. They replace words that have already been used. They:
- link ideas together without repeating nouns or phrases
- make it easier to read the text
- make the text more interesting, because when you use them, you don't have to repeat nouns or phrases.

Replace the words in italics with **it**, **they**, **he**, **him**, and then compare the new text with the old. Which one is easier to read, and more interesting? The answers are on page 60.

PRACTICE EXERCISE 6

The man ran out of the big house, carrying a bag. *The bag* was heavy, and *the man* couldn't run very fast. Suddenly, two policemen appeared around the corner and saw *the man*. *The two policemen* shouted at *the man*, and started to run after *the man*. The man dropped the bag, and one of the policemen picked *the bag* up. *The policeman* opened *the bag*, and saw that *the bag* was full of books. *The books* were very valuable, and *the books* had been stolen from the house.

The following notes were made by a reporter for the local newspaper, at a meeting of local people about plans for holding a festival in the town. The reporter is opposed to the plan. The notes need to be expanded into a short article for the newspaper. Write the article from the notes, keeping the order as given but adding any words you feel are necessary to make it clear. Try to make it as interesting as possible. There is a model answer on page 61.

PRACTICE EXERCISE 7

Three days too long.
Central Park isn't good – too many houses near, too much noise.
Parking very difficult – not enough room behind church. Parking is already difficult in town.
Business isn't needed – don't want our town full of tourists.
Local residents worried about town being too crowded.

PRACTICE EXERCISE 8

Four of the following sentences come from a *report*, and three from an *article*. Put the letters of the sentences from the *report* on the left, and those from the *article* on the right. The answers are on page 61.

a As requested, I visited the hotel in Oxford, and I enclose my comments.

b Calling all parents! Do you know that some teenagers spend 50% of their leisure time on computer games?

c Another thing for Mums and Dads to look out for is "too much tv"!

d The hotel is well situated near the centre of town, and it has ten spacious bedrooms, all with bathroom and TV.

e There is a lovely view from the hotel windows, which overlook the sea.

f Don't worry if your home seems to be a battleground at the moment. Teenagers do grow up.

g In short, I have no hesitation in recommending this hotel, and suggest that it should be included in our brochure.

Report	Article
1	1
2	2
3	3
4	

PRACTICE EXERCISE 9

You have been asked to write an article for your school magazine about the advantages of living in a town. Look at the information below and decide which you would include in the article and which you would leave out. Then write the article, expanding the information and adding connectors where necessary. You can change the order of the points if you want to. The introduction and the conclusion have been written for you.

There is a model answer on page 61.

I live in a town, and I feel that it is much better to live in a town than in the country; I would recommend living in a town for a number of reasons.

1 There are many buses in a town, so it is easy to get about.
2 The countryside is beautiful.
3 The town is very busy.
4 There are usually a lot of shops.
5 You can meet friends easily in a town.
6 It is very quiet and peaceful in the country.
7 There are usually a lot of clubs and different activities to do in a town.
8 There can be different sports facilities in a town.
9 A town may be dirty and noisy.
10 A town is often exciting and lively.

For these reasons, I would never want to live anywhere else!

How did you decide which information to leave out?

PLANNING

You need to think of ideas for your topic and write them down in a list, or in a diagram. Then you read the question again, and decide which ideas are directly related to the question and which are just about the topic but are not relevant.

Look at the following question, and the ideas below it. Which ideas are not relevant for the composition?

> You have been asked to write some points for a campaign against smoking that is being run in your area. Write a paragraph about the problems caused by smoking.
>
> 1 Friends can share cigarettes.
> 2 Smoke is unpleasant when you are eating in a restaurant.
> 3 Smoking can cause lung cancer.
> 4 Smoking stops people feeling nervous.
> 5 Cigarettes can cause fires.
> 6 Smoking is expensive.
> 7 Smoking can cause illness even in people in the same room.

Now write the paragraph, linking the ideas you have chosen in a logical way, using clear connecting words or phrases. There is a model answer on page 61.

EXAM EXERCISES

An international young people's magazine is investigating the question:
Should young people stop watching television?

Write an **article** for the magazine on this topic, based on your own experience.

Here is a sample answer to Exam Exercise 1. *Use the marking key* and try to grade it. Then read the comments.

1 Should young people stop watching television? This is the question. A lot of
  people, specially young people, spend a lot of time watching television. In
  some cases I would say too much time. At the age of sixteen to twenty one or
  twenty two you are in a moment of your life in which you have to plan your
5 future not only with the studies, also making friends, meeting people and
  having good relationships. At this age you start to find out about the life.
  You start to travel with your friends or boyfriend/girlfriend and you
  understand some of the meanings that you had never understood before. If
  you don't do this you might have problems. In the other hand sometimes
10 is good for your culture to watch the television. You can learn a lot in some
  of the programs and even films so that's not bad. Also you can use the
  television for enjoy yourself watching a film or a program or sports, what you
  like. In my opinion you have to find the way to do everything I have
  mentioned. If the television is used in the right way I think is very useful. I
15 don't think the young people should stop watching television.

Comments
You should have ticked boxes **a**, **b**, **c**, **e**, **f**, **g** in Band 3, and box **d** in Band 2.

The writer has answered the question, but his argument is quite difficult to follow.
There are several grammatical mistakes, such as:

line 5 "not only with the studies, also making friends" should be "not only with studies but also making friends"

line 6 "the life" should be "life"

line 9 "In the other hand" should be "On the other hand"

line 11 "Also you can use the television for enjoy yourself" should be "You can also use television to enjoy yourself"

line 12 what you like" should be "whatever you like"

There are some vocabulary mistakes, such as:

line 4 "in a moment of your life" should be "at a point in your life"
line 10 "culture" should be "cultural development"

It is not always easy to see what point the writer is making, although in fact he has made several good comments and there is a clear conclusion. This is mostly because there are no paragraphs, and the organisation of the ideas is poor. There should have been three paragraphs, starting in *lines 1*, *9* and *13*.

The style is appropriate, and is consistent throughout.

SAMPLE COMPOSITION 2

Now read this sample answer to the same Exam Exercise, *use the marking key* and try to grade it. Then answer the questions under the answer, which will focus on accuracy. You will find comments and answers to the questions on page 61.

1   Since the silly box was invented, the people haven't stopped being highly influenced by the programmes they see on TV. Apart from being an entertainment, it has had, in many countries, certain "colour" according to the political party which has been in power at that moment.

5   However, today that's not the problem exactly; I would say that, nowadays, the TV set is a way of "miseducating" our kids, by showing propaganda completely unsuitable for them at early hours of the day.

Afterwards, when we read a terrible happening in the newspaper, like crimes committed by children, we wonder how such an incredible thing can happen.
10   What can they learn after having seen Rambo or Terminator on TV?

I'm not saying children should stop watching TV straightaway, I do recognise that cartoons, for instance, are very enjoyable for them, and some very well done, but there are many full of violence too.

So, what about watching TV with moderation, by choosing the appropriate
15   programmes for our kids?
Let's consider TV as a way of education as well as a relaxing entertainment.

Questions

Find the mistakes in the following lines:

line 1   unnecessary article
line 4   wrong tense
line 6   wrong word
line 8   missing preposition

EXAM EXERCISE 4

An international young people's magazine is interested in finding out what kind of holiday young people prefer.

Write an article for the magazine entitled "My ideal holiday".

SAMPLE COMPOSITION 1

Here is a sample answer to Exam Exercise 4. *Use the marking key* and try to grade it. Then read the comments under the answer to see if you were right.

1   It would be so nice for me to go someplace far away from the city, from it's noise and contamination, a place where I wouldn't hear about crimes, deaths, violence or any kind of bad news.
My ideal holiday is to be in the country, where I can relax, read a book
5   and forget about work. I'd just like to be enjoying the nature, laying on the fresh grass under the trees with flowers all around me, breathing clean and fresh air, and having by my side the ones that I love, the people that love me for what I am and just the way I am, people that value such simple things as I do.
I'd like to be in a place where I could be sure that anyone who will
10   come by my side would be just the way he is. Because sometimes most of the

people that you meet don't use to be sincere at you, and just when you think that you really know someone, you discover that he was completely different from the person you thought he was.

Comments

You should have ticked all of the boxes in Band 4.

This is a full answer, with some originality, and box **a** was close to Band 5 because of this originality. However, it was not a Band 5 answer because the last part of the composition was not really relevant. It would have been better with a conclusion that returned to the idea of the ideal holiday, to focus on the question.

There are some mistakes of grammar and vocabulary, but these are minor:

line 2 "it's" should be "its"

line 4 "the nature" should be "the countryside"

line 9 "people that value such simple things as I do" should be "people who value the simple things that I do"

line 10 "come by my side" should be "coming with me"

line 11 "don't use to be sincere at you" should be "aren't usually sincere" *or* "aren't usually honest with you"

The vocabulary shows a good range, although "someplace" in *line 1* is more common in American English.

The style is quite informal, for example in the use of contractions (I'd) but this is all right in an article.

Now read this sample answer to the same Exam Exercise, *use the marking key* and try to grade it. Then answer the question, which focuses on organisation.

SAMPLE COMPOSITION 2

1   When I thought about my ideal holiday, I thought about which place would I want to go. But I couldn't choose one place because I want to go round the world.
     If I would go round the world, I would start from China to see the
5   "Great Wall" and walk down there.
     Next, I would go to Thailand and lie on the beach.
     And I would go to India to see a Gandis river. There would be a lot of people who purify their spirit and soul.
     Then I would go Africa and I'd like to see wild animals – lions,
10   panthers, elephants and etc.
     After shopping in Europe, I would go to United States to hear music.
     There would be so many kinds of music. for example Jazz, Rhythm and Blues, Rock 'n' Roll. Listening to music would be happy for me.
     If I would go round world, I could grow up. I would see people, scenes
15   buildings and hear other language and music, I would be changed my self. I hope to be that.
     That is my ideal holiday.

Question

This composition has too many paragraphs, and needs to have connecting words to make the answer complete instead of just a collection of ideas. Rewrite the composition in five paragraphs, adding connectors where necessary. You can change the order of the sentences if you want to. Be careful with the conditional sentence in *line 4*, and with the meaning in *lines 13* and *16*.

There is an improved answer on page 61.

One of the compositions for you to choose from in Part 2 is often a story. Stories are usually a sequence of actions, usually in the past tense. When you plan your story, you need to make sure that the sequence of actions is clear, and easy to follow.

CONNECTING ACTIONS

Actions are usually connected by using *sequencing words*, such as:
> *then*
> *after that*
> *suddenly*
> *soon*
> *first, second, third*
> *in the end*
> *in the beginning*

These are the signposts in the narrative that help the reader to keep the events clear in time.

You can also use words that show the writer's attitude – these show how the writer is feeling about the events:
> *unfortunately*
> *sadly*
> *luckily*
> *happily*

A story often follows a pattern:
• background information and scene setting
• first actions
• later actions or consequences
• final result

Each section of the story should be in a different paragraph.

PLANNING

If you are asked to write a short story called "*The day that everything went wrong*", you should plan the events in sequence. Here is an example:

1 Woke up late.
2 Hurried to station to catch train.
3 Missed train. Had to wait one hour for next one.
4 Late for work. Missed important meeting.
5 Boss very angry.
6 Went home. Missed last bus from station and had to walk.

You should then think about which tenses to use, and how to connect each event.
For example,
> "When I arrived at the station, the train had just left."
> "As I returned home, I was feeling very unhappy."

You should then think about adding interest; for example, how I felt while hurrying to the station, what the boss said, and so on.

Put the following actions into a sequence. The answer is on page 62.

a We had to watch the match on TV.

b On the big day we left home by car, feeling very excited because we had been looking forward to going to the football match for a long time.

c We waited for three hours, unable to move.

d We drove for an hour without any problems, but then we reached the town where the match was going to be played.

e We turned round and went home.

f There were hundreds of cars all going the same way, and suddenly we got stuck in a traffic jam only 30 minutes away from the ground.

g Our team lost anyway!

MAKING YOUR STORY MORE INTERESTING

One of the most important things you need to do when writing a story is to keep the interest of the reader, and to make the story interesting and exciting.

Read the two extracts below, and decide which one is the most interesting and why. Mark the words in the text that created an atmosphere of interest and suspense.

1 The boy walked into the room. He looked around, and saw that he was alone; he didn't know what to do, so he walked to the window and looked out. He saw a man walking across the grass towards the house, and suddenly felt afraid. He didn't know who the man was, but he was sure he was dangerous.

2 The small boy crept silently into the room, glancing around suspiciously as he did so. With a feeling of relief, he realised that he was alone. He couldn't decide what to do, so he ran to the large open window and stared out. He glimpsed a tall, dark man hiding near the part of the house where he was, and he suddenly felt terrified. He had no idea who the man was, but he was sure he was extremely dangerous.

The more interesting text uses adjectives and adverbs, to give more atmosphere and to hold the reader's interest. These words also give more information – you know that the boy is small, for example.

You should try to use adjectives and adverbs in your stories, and also words that say exactly what you want, like "glancing". For example,

"The man *walked* along the road" only tells you *where* he went, but

"The man *limped* along the road" tells you *how* he walked, and is more interesting.

Here are some exercises with suggestions for more interesting words to use in stories. The answers to all these Practice Exercises are on page 62.

Use the nouns in capitals to form an adjective or adverb which fits suitably in the blank space. Fill each blank in this way.

1 The novel was so _____ that he couldn't put it down.
   EXCITEMENT

2 The man drove so _____ that he had ten accidents in three months.
   CARE

3 The ghost in that castle is so _____ that no-one will visit it at night.
   TERROR

4 The prisoner escaped by walking _____ out of the back door of the court building.
   SILENCE

5 "Give me your money, or I'll kill you", the robber shouted _____ .
THREAT

6 The news about the earthquake was so _____ that we were all in tears.
DEPRESSION

7 I can't remember when I've seen such a _____ film before.
THRILL

8 The noise from the factory is so _____ that no-one wants to sit in the garden before 5pm.
DEAFNESS

PRACTICE EXERCISE 3

There are many different verbs that you can use to avoid repeating words in a story, and to be more precise in what you want to say.

Replace the gaps with the following words, changing the form when necessary.

Ways of walking

creep   *rush*   *limp*   *march*

1 The thief _____ into the house, trying not to be seen.
2 The football player _____ off the pitch after hurting his knee.
3 The band _____ into town at the front of the parade.
4 The students all _____ out of the classroom at the end of the last lesson on Friday afternoon.

Ways of looking

stare   *glance*   *frown*   *watch*

1 The man waiting at the bus stop kept _____ impatiently at his watch.
2 The family seemed to spend a lot of time _____ television.
3 The student found it difficult to concentrate in the exam, and spent a lot of time _____ out of the window.
4 The librarian _____ angrily at the students who were making a noise in the library.

Ways of speaking

whisper   *shout*   *scream*   *call*

1 As the woman saw the man with a knife, she _____ in terror.
2 The two students at the back of the class were not paying attention, but were _____ quietly to each other.
3 The shop assistant _____ at the thief to stop, but he ran away.
4 When the baby was born, her parents _____ her Maria.

Try to use some of the words from the exercises in sentences of your own.

EXPANDING VOCABULARY

There are some words that are used so often that they lose their real meaning; these are words that can be used for anything, such as:

fantastic
great
wonderful
terrific

You can have a fantastic film, book, meal, friend, or football game!

One of the words to avoid if possible in your story is "nice", as this is used too often and is not very interesting to read.

Try to replace the word *nice* in the following description with a word that is more interesting. Choose from the words below, but you can't use a word more than once! There is one word that you will *not* need to use. The answer is on page 62.

comfortable   friendly   soft   funny   wonderful   difficult   luxurious   delicious

When we went on holiday last year, we had a *nice* time. We travelled in a very *nice* bus with a really *nice* driver, who told us *nice* stories that made us laugh.

The hotel room was *nice*, with its own bathroom and sitting area; the food in the restaurant was *nice*, and the hotel band played *nice* music during the meal, so it was very romantic.

I'm looking forward to going back there next year!

EXAM EXERCISES

You have decided to enter a short-story competition. The competition rules say that the story must begin or end with the following words:

"Elizabeth closed the door slowly behind her, and suddenly started to smile."

Write your **story** for the competition.

Here is a sample answer to Exam Exercise 1. *Use the marking key* and try to grade it. Then read the comments under the answer to see if you were right.

1   It was Sunday the 23rd December. Everything was covered with wonderful, white snow. All last night it had been snowing and it was the first white Christmas since several years.
    Elizabeth, a little child of 6 years, had been playing with her favourite toys. In
5   her play she was a mother of a teddybear and a baby. She liked to play this game again and again. But this time her mind had the Christmas tree and the gifts. She knew her gift was the biggest present of all and it was in red paper with a golden flower made of paper on it. The door to the salon was open and she could see a few branches of the tree. While she had been playing she
10 looked all the time through the corridor into the living room. "What a wonderful tree!" But her present was more interesting. She couldn't stop herself any longer. She had to know what inside the parcel was. Anything for her doll's house? A new dress for her Barbie? She got up, walked very silently to the door, looked for her parents, crossed the corridor and went into the
15 living room. After that she took her present and shaked it. Nothing, no noise. She held it against the light and she could see the sign of ... Now she was very happy and she put the gift back under the tree and went to the door. Elizabeth closed the door slowly behind her, and suddenly started to smile.

Comments

You should have ticked boxes **b, c, d, e** in Band 4, and **a, f, g** in Band 5.

This is a good answer, which answers the question fully and has some original ideas. The writer has introduced a variety of sentence structures – the use of questions in *line 13* and the direct speech in *line 10* involve the reader directly in the story and add interest.

There are only a few grammatical mistakes, which do not prevent understanding:
    line 3 "since several years" should be "for several years"
    line 15 "shaked" should be "shook"

There is a word order problem in *line 12*: "what inside the parcel was" should be "what was inside the parcel".

The writer has tried to make the story interesting by adding colourful descriptions, as in:
  lines 1-2 "covered with wonderful, white snow"
  line 7 "in red paper with a golden flower made of paper on it".

There are also some wrong words, but these do not prevent understanding:
  line 5 "play" should be "game"
  line 8 "salon" should be "living room"

The story leads clearly to the last line, which follows the sequence of events logically. The first paragraph gives clear background, and also introduces the atmosphere of the story. However the paragraphing is not always clear: there could have been another paragraph in *line 13* "She got up", and again in *line 18* "Elizabeth closed the door".

The style of the writing is always appropriate.

SAMPLE COMPOSITION 2

Now read this sample answer to the same Exam Exercise, ***use the marking key*** and try to grade it. Then answer the questions under the answer, which will focus on accuracy. You will find comments and answers to the questions on page 62.

1   Elizabeth closed the door slowly behind her, and suddenly started to smile. Two days ago, the teacher told her that her marks at school had been so bad and that she would fail the year. At this time, everything had gone wrong for her. Elizabeth had hated this girl from the beginning. She was prettier and
5   more intelligent than her. And that, she had never accepted it.

Quickly, and with the help of Clark (unfortunately he wasn't Superman, not even super!) they had planned a very simple deed: Clark was going to occupy the teacher with having a drink and at the same time, she was going to enter in "Big Brother", the college's computer, and correct the marks. For that, a
10   date had been decided: it would be two days later.

On "D Day", Elizabeth had gone to the teacher's desk, had turned on the computer and had corrected the marks. When she had gone out, Elizabeth had been very quiet, even not a little shake. It had been so simple!
After that, she had met another student in the corridor, he had been so
15   excited that she had asked him what had been going on. And the student had answered: "Clark and Mrs. Bowl, you know her, she's your teacher! They had been killed!"

She had gone to her room, had closed the door slowly behind her and suddenly started to laugh. It had been so simple!

Questions
Find and correct the following mistakes:
  line 5   unnecessary pronoun
  line 8   wrong preposition
  line 9   unnecessary preposition
  line 11 two wrong tenses
  line 12 two wrong tenses
  line 14 two wrong tenses
  line 15 wrong tense
  line 16 wrong tense
  line 17 wrong tense
  line 18 two wrong tenses

A national newspaper is holding a short story competition. The competition rules say that you must include at least six of the following eight words or phrases:

EXAM EXERCISE 2

a cruel giant	*a princess*	*a magic sword*	*a dark palace*
a wicked uncle	*a deep lake*	*a dark stranger*	*the wedding day*

Write your **story** for the competition.

Here is a sample answer to Exam Exercise 2. *Use the marking key* and try to grade it. Then read the comments under the answer to see if you were right.

SAMPLE COMPOSITION 1

1 Once upon a time, there was a big kingdom. It had a good king, called King
    Charles. He wife, Queen Helen was a beautiful woman, but she died in the
    birth of their daughter, the princess Anne. In this kingdom, nobody suffered
    from hunger or poorness, because King Charles was very fair to his people.
5   Near, was the King John's kingdom. These two kingdoms were very friends
    and helped each other in problems and difficulties. Between them, was a deep
    lake, which was believed of having inside of it a cruel giant. It was the
    symbol of this friendship. King John and princess Anne fell in love and they
    wanted to get married. The wedding day came, but it didn't happen. Suddenly
10 a dark grey cloud covered the sun and all people of both kingdom slept deeply.
    Less the princess and King John. After a bad witch appeared and separated
    them. She sent the princess to a dark palace and said him that she, the witch,
    wanted to marry him. He was very angry, so he took her magic sword and
    killed her pressing it against her heart. After, everything became normal and
15 the king and the princess got married.

Comments

You should have ticked boxes **a**, **b**, **c**, **f**, **g** in Band 3, and boxes **d**, **e** in Band 2.

Six of the words have been used and so the writer has fulfilled the task, although the story does not have any real detail. The sentences are all quite simple, with little variety. However, the spelling is good.

There are several grammatical mistakes which sometimes cause difficulty in understanding:
    line 4 "poorness" should be "poverty"
    line 7 "which was believed of having" should be "which was believed to have"
    line 11 "Less the princess" which should be "Except the princess"

The story is not very easy to follow because there are not many sequencing words to help, and "after" is used incorrectly – should be "after that". When there is a sequencing word used such as "Suddenly" in *line 9*, it is good. More often, however, the actions are just added on one after the other.

The style is appropriate – the beginning is very good, and exactly right for this kind of story, which is a fairy tale.

Letts

SAMPLE COMPOSITION 2

Now read this sample answer to the same Exam Exercise, *use the marking key* and try to grade it. Then answer the questions under the answer, which will focus on accuracy. You will find comments and answers to the questions on page 63.

1   Before I am going to tell you the short story I will give you some information about my characters. Aria is a princess. Her eyes shine like diamonds. Macho is a dark stranger and Omach is a wicked uncle. Finally, there is a magic butterfly, Raia.

5   Once upon a time there was an immense garden in Scotland with a palace and a deep lake. Aria lived in this palace and Raia was her bosom friend. Yes, she was a special friend. Aria often daydreamed the wedding day and the dark knight who would have taken away. This idea helped her to overcome the vexations of her wicked uncle.

10   The days were spending slow when a dark stranger arrived at the palace. Macho was his name. He sang the legend of Potame, a magic sword and Aria felt strange emotions and a great excitement.

Aria spent a sleepless night and when she was falling asleep, Macho waked up her with a kiss. She understood Macho was her dark knight. She decided
15   to flee with him and Raia helped them. So Aria had realised her dream at last.

Questions

Find and correct the following mistakes:

line 1   wrong tense
line 7   missing preposition
line 8   missing pronoun
line 10 wrong verb/adverb form needed
line 13 wrong tense/wrong form of past tense

EXAM EXERCISE 3

Your local library is running a competition for the best short **story** written on the subject of *"A holiday friendship"*. Write your entry for the competition.

SAMPLE COMPOSITION 1

Here is a sample answer to Exam Exercise 3. *Use the marking key* and try to grade it. Then read the comments under the answer to see if you were right.

1   One day last summer, I decided to go on holiday on my own, so I packed my rucksack and started my adventure. I headed for Valencia, which is in the east coast of Spain, and has the best beaches.

However, my holiday suddenly went wrong when a rough-looking man
5   came up and threatened me by a knife. He wanted me give him money, but I had left most of it at the youth hostel so he took my watch and my rings and then ran away.

On the next few days I was difficult to relax and wondered about going home when my luck changed. In a disco, I asked a young man to light my
10   cigarette. He was tall and handsome with fair hair and blue eyes. We talked together and started to fall in love. It was love at first glance.

We met on the beach every day and spend our time swimming and sunbathing. In the evenings we went to the disco where we first met.

My holiday in Valencia had a terible start, but a wonderful happy end!

Comments

You should have ticked boxes **a, b, c, e, f, g** in Band 4, and **d** in Band 5.

The writer has answered the question with enough detail, and used a good range of grammatical structures, although there are some mistakes. They are generally minor, and it is not difficult to understand the storyline.

The mistakes are:

line 3 "in the east coast" should be "on the east coast"

line 5 "by a knife" should be "with a knife"

line 5 "he wanted me give him money" should be "he wanted me to give him money"

line 8 "On the next few days I was difficult to relax" should be "During the next few days it was difficult to relax"

line 11 "love at first glance" should be "love at first sight"

line 12 "spend our time " should be "spent our time"

There is some interesting vocabulary, such as "a rough-looking man" in *line 4*, and some good expressions, such as "my luck changed" in *line 9*.

The presentation is excellent, with very clear paragraphs which set out the storyline well, and the style is right for this type of writing.

Now read the following answer to the same Exam Exercise, and the comments underneath. Then rewrite the composition to improve the standard, changing the underlined sections and taking into account what the comments said. There is an improved version on page 63.

SAMPLE COMPOSITION 2

1   What a boring holiday! Susan thought to herself. <u>At the first wonderful,</u>
     <u>but at the last it had been horrible, and she never thought that she spent a lot</u>
     <u>of money.</u>
        She had met a nice boy called <u>tom</u> quite early on, but <u>they liked each</u>
5   <u>other, they were still shy.</u> <u>After that,</u> she decided to have a last swim before
     lunch. When she had finished swimming, she went to a restaurant alone <u>for to</u>
     <u>take her lunch, then</u> she returned to the beach, but she had eaten a lot so she
     wanted to have a siesta. <u>She laid near the sea and after she went swiming,</u>
     <u>then she fell under the sea.</u>
10   <u>When tom saw her and help her from the sea.</u> When <u>susan</u> opened her
     eyes she saw <u>tom near her</u> and <u>it started new life between them.</u> Susan gazed
     into <u>tom's</u> eyes. She could hardly believe that <u>she had got the crown of her</u>
     <u>dream with the man who steel love her and never give up between them.</u>

Comments

This answer would be in Band 2.

There are many careless mistakes, such as spelling, punctuation and grammar. The incorrect use of connecting words and tenses makes it difficult for the reader to understand exactly what the writer means. There are some things that do not seem to have any purpose – for example, the money in *line 3*.

The composition needs to be more connected, with reasons given for why she "fell under the sea". The events could be made more interesting, with more use of connectors and sequencing words, and more reasons for why the holiday had been horrible in the first paragraph.

Exam tip

Make sure you have enough time to read your composition carefully when you have finished writing it, so that you can correct any careless mistakes (see *Timing* on page 2).

EXAM EXERCISE 4 Your teacher has asked you to write a short story for the school magazine. The title of the story is "*The Robbery*". Write the **story**.

SAMPLE COMPOSITION 1

Here is a sample answer to Exam Exercise 4. *Use the marking key* and try to grade it. Then read the comments under the answer to see if you were right.

1   Last Saturday I went to London to make shopping. I needed a lot of different
     things, so I went to Harrods because there I can find everything I need.
     In the middle of the day, something happened. Ten men with mask and gun
     came to the shop and start to take everything they can. Everybody was
5   desperate and we lay on the floor and couldn't move. At that moment, I
     started to cry and I was sure that was only the beginner.
     Then, I started to listen some different noisy. After a minute I knew it was the
     police. The thieves went crazy and they wanted kill everybody, but the police
     were really quickly and in five minutes everything was finished. After all this, I
10   came back to my house and I swear never come back to Harrods.

Comments

You should have ticked boxes **b**, **c**, **d**, **e**, **g** in Band 2, and **a**, **f** in Band 3.

This could have been an interesting story, but there is not enough detail, and there are too many mistakes. They are:

line 1 "to make shopping" should be "to go shopping"
line 3 "ten men with mask and gun" should be "ten men with masks and guns"
line 4 "start to take everything they can" should be "started to take everything they could"
line 6 "beginner" should be "beginning"
line 7 "listen some different noisy" should be "hear some different noises"
line 8 "wanted kill" should be "wanted to kill"
line 9 "quickly" should be "quick" (you cannot use an adverb form with the verb "to be")
line 10 should be "I went back to my house and swore never to go back to Harrods".

The presentation could be improved with a line between the paragraphs to make them clear, as it looks as if it is just one paragraph. The style is basically right for this kind of writing.

SAMPLE COMPOSITION 2

Now read this sample answer to the same Exam Exercise, *use the marking key* and try to grade it. Then answer the questions, which will focus on making the writing interesting. You will find comments and answers to the questions on page 63.

1   One day, as soon as I got back to my house from work, I found that
     somebody had broken into my house while I was out. I was too surprised to
     do anything when I found it, so I was just standing and thinking what I should
     do next. After a few minutes, I phoned the police. Then I was checking what
5   the robber had stolen from my house. I found that the robber had stolen my
     credit card, my rings which were made of gold, some china which had been
     very difficult to collect and some expensive clothes. Then the police arrived
     and they asked me for some details of the robbery. They said they would tell
     me if they found out who the robber was.
10   A few days later I received a telephone call from the police, and I was
     so shocked that I couldn't say anything at all. It was my neighbour!

Questions

1 Which lines show how the writer feels?
2 The writer has not told us: a) how she felt when she was checking what had been stolen; b) how she felt while waiting for the police to catch the robber. And some words to *lines 4/5* and *line 9* to fill in this missing information. **Note:** the composition has already got 155 words, so you can only add about 25 more.

You may be asked to write two letters in the exam, one in Part 1 and one in Part 2. Part 1 is the compulsory question, so you must answer it; it is often formal or semi-formal. There is help with answering this Part 1 question in Chapter 2. The second letter may be in Part 2, and you can choose whether to answer it or not. It may be:

- a formal letter, such as a letter of application for a job or a course of study
- an informal letter, such as a letter to a friend.

PLANNING

You will always be given the situation clearly in the question, and you must make sure that you complete every part of the question. You will lose marks if you do not do everything that the question asks you to do, because you will not have fulfilled the task.

You do not need to include an address at the top of the letter unless the question asks you to do so.

Formal letters

Formal letters always follow a pattern:

1 Greeting
2 Reason for writing the letter
3 Background information
4 Further details, or more information
5 Any requests you want to make
6 Ending the letter

You should start a new paragraph when you start a new section.

Here is a letter of application, with these sections clearly marked for you.

1 [Dear Sir,

2 [I am writing to apply for the job of sports officer which was advertised in the newspaper yesterday.

3 [I am 25 years old, and I have just finished a degree course in English. I have always enjoyed sports, and during my university holidays I have worked as an assistant in summer camps like yours.

4 [I can play football, tennis and basketball; furthermore, I am qualified to teach both sailing and canoeing.

5 [Could you please send me further details of the job, including the salary?

6 [I look forward to hearing from you.
Yours faithfully,

Formal letters may be written indented, as above, or blocked, as below. If you block your letter, remember to leave a line between the paragraphs.

1 [Dear Sir,

2 [I am writing to apply for the job of sports officer which was advertised in the newspaper yesterday.

3 [I am 25 years old, and I have just finished a degree course in English. I have always enjoyed sports, and during my university holidays I have worked as an assistant in summer camps like yours.

4 [I can play football, tennis and basketball; furthermore, I am qualified to teach both sailing and canoeing.

5 [Could you please send me further details of the job, including the salary?

6 [I look forward to hearing from you.

Yours faithfully,

Formal letters may also include set phrases, which appear in different parts of the letter. Here are some examples, which may be useful to learn and use.

Reason for writing: *I am writing to ...*
                       With reference to your letter, I would like to ...

Background: *Furthermore ...*
                       In addition to this, I ...

Requests: *I would be grateful if you could ...*
                       Would it be possible for you to ...

Ending: *I look forward to hearing from you.*

Be careful to start and end your letter correctly, as there are set phrases for this.

Start	**End**
Dear Sir, Dear Madam,	Yours faithfully,
Dear Mr. Brown, *(a man)* Dear Mrs. Brown, *(a married woman)* Dear Ms. Brown, *(a woman who may be married or not)* Dear Miss Brown, *(an unmarried woman)*	Yours sincerely,
Dear John, Dear Mary,	Best wishes,

Informal letters

An informal letter does not have to follow the same set pattern, although it does also have certain conventions. It should include

1 Greeting
2 Reason for writing
3 Details and further information
4 Final comments
5 Ending

You do not need to include an address unless the question asks you to.

Informal letters are usually written in indented format. They do not usually include set phrases, but you can use:
• contractions, e.g. *They're leaving home tomorrow.*
• phrasal verbs, e.g. *I'll pick you up at the station.* ("pick up" means "collect")
• exclamation marks: !

Here are some ideas for phrases to include in an informal letter.

Reason for writing: *I haven't seen you for a long time!*
                       I'm writing to ask a favour.

Ending: *I hope I'll see you soon.*
                       Please write soon.
                       I'm looking forward to hearing from you.

Remember to include all the information you have been asked for in the question, otherwise you will not fulfill the task.

PUNCTUATION

There are some conventions that you should try to follow with your use of punctuation. Here are some basic rules to help you.

Capital letters (G)
- start a sentence
- are always used with names
- are used to start direct speech

Full stops (.)
- end a sentence

Commas (,)
- come at the end of phrases
- link ideas
- come after linking words such as "however"
- separate items in a list
- come after the greeting in a letter and after the ending phrase

Semi-colons (;)
- break a sentence when a full stop is not necessary because the idea is continued

Colons (:)
- come before the start of a list
- stand in place of "because"

Apostrophes (')
- are used with possession ("Jill's book")
- show that a letter is missing in a negative (*don't = do not*) or a contraction (*I've = I have*)

Exclamation marks (!)
- are used in informal letters to show emotion
- are used in direct speech

Note: try not to use exclamation marks too often.

Question marks (?)
- come after questions

1 The following letter has been written without paragraphing or punctuation. Rewrite the letter, putting in paragraphs and punctuation. The answer is on page 63.

> dear jane i am writing to thank you for the great party last week it was really enjoyable and it was nice to see all my old friends again im looking forward to seeing you again next month at the school reunion could you please bring some things for me that i cant find here id like some tea coffee and an english grammar book by the way i met john last week and he asked me to say hi to you with thanks and best wishes mary

2 Now find 12 mistakes in punctuation in the following letter. The answer is on page 63.

> Dear Sue,
>   guess who I saw last week – James! Hed been to visit Janes' friend Peter, and I bumped into him quite by chance in the pub He was really well, and told me to say "Hi to you. Hes going to france next week to start a new job there, so I suppose we wont see him for some time
>   I just thought youd be interested.
>   See you soon
>   love,
>   Andrew

PRACTICE EXERCISE 1

PRACTICE EXERCISE 2

Here is an example of a formal letter and an informal letter, but they are mixed up. Separate the two letters, and then write both letters in full, using either indented or blocked style. The answer is on page 63.

a Dear Mary,

b Dear Sir,

c I am writing to ask for further information about the evening course in French, which was advertised in "The Telegraph" yesterday.

d I look forward to hearing from you.

e It was great to see you last week, but I forgot to ask you something so I'm writing now!

f I am looking for an intensive course, and your advertisement seemed to be just what I need.

g I'm really looking forward to seeing you again.

h I'd be grateful if you could send me a brochure, with information about your school.

i Could you give me Peter's address? I've lost it, and I need to contact him. You could give it to me when we meet next week.

j Thanks a lot!

k Yours faithfully,

l Best wishes,

EXAM EXERCISES

EXAM EXERCISE 1

CITY MUSEUM

'School visits officer' required. Mornings only.
Duties - to welcome school groups,
          - to show them round the museum.

Interested in local history?
Like answering difficult questions?
Can you bring the past to life?

To apply, write us a letter explaining why you are the best person for the job!

Write your **letter of application** to the City Museum Curator. Do not write any addresses.

SAMPLE COMPOSITION 1

Here is a sample answer to Exam Exercise 1. *Use the marking key* and try to grade it. Then read the comments to see if you were right.

1   Dear Sir or Madam,
    I am writing to you because of the advertising I read on the newspaper today,
    about the schools visitor required.
    I understood immediately it was treating a perfect job for me.
5   I have just finished my university in history and I am practitioner in a primary
    school in London. So I am improving myself to be communicative and able to
    arouse interest about history and the past.
    I believe the past has to be present and live between us, exactly like you said in
    your advertising.
10 I specialize in local history as well because I am really interested to know our
    origins and back-culture, to pass them on to people, but above all to children
    and young students because they will be our future.

Finally I can say I am the right person to get this job for my interests, skills, preparation and passion in it.

15 I will be grateful to you to give me a chance to express my abilities in a so wonderful context like the City Museum.

Yours faithfully,

Comments

You should have ticked boxes **a**, **c**, **d**, **f** in Band 3, and boxes **b**, **e**, **g** in Band 2.

The writer has answered the question, and there is a satisfactory range of structures including:

line 10 "I specialize in local history"

line 11 "above all to children and young students because they will be our future".

The range of vocabulary is wide, including:

line 7 "arouse interest"

line 11 "to pass them on to people"

However, there are numerous errors in both structure and vocabulary that do not communicate clearly to the reader. These include:

line 2 "I read on the newspaper today" should be "I read in the newspaper today"

line 4 "it was treating a perfect job for me" should be "it was a perfect job for me"

line 5 "I am practitioner in a primary school" should be "I am working in a primary school"

line 8 "the past has to be present and live between us" needs to be completely rewritten, and should be "the past has to be related to the present"

line 10 "I am really interested to know our origins and back-culture" should be "I am really interested in knowing our origins and background"

line 13 "I am the right person to get this job for my interests, skills, preparation and passion in it" should be "I am the right person for this job because of my interest and ability to handle the subject"

The paragraphs are not clearly organised, and there are too many for the ideas given. You should look at the format at the beginning of this chapter for some ideas on how to paragraph this letter. The writer uses connecting words, e.g. "finally", and the style is exactly right for this type of letter.

Now read this sample answer to the same Exam Exercise, *use the marking key* and try to grade it. Then answer the questions, which will focus on accuracy. You will find comments and answers to the questions on page 64.

SAMPLE
COMPOSITION 2

1 To the City Museum Curator
My name is Sue Robinson and I am 48 years old.
Today I saw your advertisement in the newspaper "School visits officer required" and I became interested immediately. I have been looking for a new
5 job for about half a year but this is the first time I have applied for a job.
At the moment I am employed at a lawyers office as a secretary.
The last twenty years I have been working there and now I feel that I need some change in my life.
In my younger days I worked at an after-school centre as a teacher and I have
10 always loved children because they are impulsive. Like answering difficult questions? Yes, and I am sure that I can do it in an exciting way so the pupils feel that they have a good time but also learned something about the past.
My husband is a historian and therefore I know a lot about the local history.
I will be very flexible concerning working hours because both of my children
15 now are grown-ups. I would be pleased to come to an interview when it is convenient to you.

Yours sincerely.

Questions

1 Find and correct the following mistakes:
   line 7   word order
   line 12 tense (2)
   line 15 word order

2 Which sentences are not written in the right style?

EXAM EXERCISE 2

Your English pen friend has asked you about the kind of books young people like reading for pleasure. Write a **letter** to your penfriend describing a book you have enjoyed reading in your free time. Describe the main events, say what was particularly exciting or interesting, and why you enjoyed it.

SAMPLE COMPOSITION 1

Here is a sample answer to Exam Exercise 2. *Use the marking key* and try to grade it. Then read the comments to see if you were right.

1   Dear John,
         Thank you for your letter. It was very interesting.
         The books I enjoy reading most is Japanese historical novels. The
     reason I started reading them is I thought they have one of the keys which
5   discovers myself. When I began reading them, I was kind of shocked because
     they point out what Japanese people are like to be, I realised I carry this
     history and I am proud of them.
         Japanese history not only reminds me of it, but also I am keen on the
     process of stories. Most stories are set in the changing era. I especially enjoy
10 reading the story about Bakumatsu-era, which is fifteen years from American
     Commodore Perry came to Japan to let us open our country in 1853 to Meiji
     Restoration in 1868.
         I read the books over and over again and am never bored. They are
     well worthwhile reading among foreigners as well as Japanese.
15   I hope this information is useful.
         Best wishes,
         Keiko

Comments

You should have ticked boxes **a**, **b**, **c**, **d**, **g** in Band 3, and **e**, **f** in Band 2.

Some of the errors in structure include:
   line 4/5 "I thought they have one of the keys which discovers myself" should be "I
             thought they would give me a key to my identity."
   line 6   "what Japanese people are like to be" should be "what Japanese people are like"
   line 7   "I am proud of them" should be "I am proud of it"
   line 9   "process of stories" should be "process of these stories"
   line 14 "among foreigners" should be "by foreigners"

The paragraphs and organisation of the ideas are satisfactory, and there are a few connecting words such as "when" and "also". There are good examples of referring words, e.g.
   line 4   "them" (Japanese historical novels)
   line 5   "them" (Japanese historical novels)
   line 13 "they" (the books – Japanese historical novels)

However, the style is rather too formal for this type of writing, and there are not enough personal references to the friend.

Now read this sample answer to the same Exam Exercise, *use the marking key* and try to grade it. Then answer the questions, which will focus on accuracy. You will find comments and answers to the questions on page 64.

SAMPLE COMPOSITION 2

1   Dear Paul,
       Hallo! How are you? I'm fine, and here everything is OK. I had just
    read a delightful book when I received your letter where you asked me
    about any book that I've enjoyed reading.
5   This book which is about people is called "People by and large". It starts
    talking the good and bad things in each part of the life, since the teenager till
    the old age. The interesting is that while it discusses a serious subject like the
    responsabilities which you have to acquire when you became adult, it show you
    the way to start this new stage of life doing the best choices.
10   The second part of the book describes more than 5 kinds of people and
    it's exciting when you find something that coincide with your own personality.
    Then you can see your qualities, your defects and try to mend one's ways.
       But I like reading this book especially because more than a book it is a
    guide which is useful for whole of my life.
15   I think you can find it at any bookshop and I'm sure you'll like the book
    as much as I.
       I hope I'll see you soon. Write to me!
       Best wishes,
          Carol

Questions

Find and correct the following mistakes:

1 *lines 5-10* are very difficult to understand, because of mistakes in structure and vocabulary. Rewrite them, changing the underlined words.

This book which is about people is called "People by and large". It starts <u>talking</u> the good and bad <u>things in each part of the life, since the teenager till the old age</u>. <u>The interesting</u> is that <u>while it discusses</u> a serious subject like the responsabilities <u>which you have to acquire when you became</u> adult, <u>it show</u> you the way to start this new stage of life <u>doing</u> the best choices.

2 *line 16* missing verb

EXAM EXERCISE 3

Your teacher has been unwell for the last two weeks. Write her a **letter** telling her what your group has been doing during this time, and offering to go and visit her soon.

Here is a sample answer to Exam Exercise 3. *Use the marking key* and try to grade it. Then read the comments to see if you were right.

SAMPLE COMPOSITION 1

1   Dear Mr. Jones,
       How are you? How is everything with you? I hope it's good. I am fine
    and all your students are good but they are asking about your health.
       Last week a new teacher came to our class his name is Smith and he is
5   55 years old. He is from South England. He looks serious all the lesson but
    actuality he is a good teacher. He can explain anything and give details.
    Yesterday, I visited him at his home and I saw the diffrent for his personality
    in the school and outsaid the school. In the school he was serious but out the
    school he looks friendly and kind.
10   Finally, I am sorry because until now I did come to visit you but I
    promise I will visit you as soon as possible.
       Yours sincerely,

Comments

You should have ticked boxes **a**, **b**, **d**, **e**, **f**, **g** in Band 3, and **c** in Band 2.

This answer has covered all the basic points, and the use of questions in the first paragraph is interesting to read. However, there are several important grammar, punctuation and spelling mistakes. These include:

line 4   the punctuation should be: "Last week, a new teacher came to our class. His name is Smith, and he is 55 years old."

line 7   "diffrent for his personality" should be "difference between his personality"

line 8   "outsaid the school" should be "outside school"

line 10 is difficult to understand because there is a negative missing, and the tense is wrong; it should be: "until now I haven't come to visit you"

Spelling – the words should be spelled as follows:

line 6   actually

line 7   difference

line 8   outside

However, the paragraphing is clear with a good indented layout, and the greeting and the ending are both appropriate. The style is mostly right for this type of writing.

SAMPLE COMPOSITION 2

Now read this sample answer to the same Exam Exercise, *use the marking key* and try to grade it. Then answer the questions, which will focus on content and style. You will find comments and answers to the questions on page 64.

1   Dear Teacher,

     I knew you have been unwell the last weeks. During your absence the new teacher has explained the conditional and we have done a lot of exercises; we went to the language lab to listen a dialogue on telephone and we had to

5   complete a test.

     Once a week we have to bring some newspapers to the classroom and to read a cultural article about review of books, museums, art exhibitions, films, theatrical show and musicals. We must underline the unknown words. After reading we make a report about the articles. The last week we improved our

10   knowledge of grammar and we made a test about passive and phrasal verbs: this was very difficult! It's better not to speak about!

     But the day after we enjoyed a very nice and interesting experience: we made by ourselves a video! I was the director and I had to organise all steps. I felt very important and a group of four people made the showman and

15   other people had been interviewed as starwomen and actors.

     You'll see it soon, because we are going to visit you at this week-end and we will show you the film. Are you happy? We'll phone you to confirm Friday evening.

     Yours sincerely,

Questions

1   Compare this answer with the first answer to this question. Which is the most interesting? Why?

2   Make a list of all the information given about the class's activities. Notice how this information lifts the standard of the answer.

3   Note all the feelings that the writer gives about the activities. These help to make the letter more personal, and therefore more interesting.

4   There are some mistakes:

line 4   missing preposition/missing article

line 9   unnecessary word

line 10 wrong verb/word missing

line 11 word missing

line 13 word order

You have just read this in an international young people's magazine.

> ## LANGUAGE LEARNING
>
> - *Evening classes?*
> - *Listening to cassettes at home or in the car?*
> - *Living in the country for six months?*
> - *Having a private teacher?*
> - *Your own system of learning?*
>
> **Which is the best way of learning a language?**

Write a **letter** to the editor, giving your opinion. Try to support your point of view with examples from your own experience.

Here is a sample answer to Exam Exercise 4. *Use the marking key* and try to grade it. Then read the comments to see if you were right.

1 Dear Sir
I think one of the most successful ways of learning a foreign language is living
for several months in the country which speaks that language. Practising is the
only method to obtain a fluent capacity of speaking, and nobody but a native
5 speaker can give you the correct accent and pronunciation.
The advantages this situation gives you are a lot and very useful: not only are
you always forced to speak that language, but you also have to think that way,
which would be impossible in your own country.
Anyway, though nothing can be compared to a direct experience of a
10 language, not everyone can incur such expenses.
Other excellent ways of learning are tapes listening, attending evening schools
or studying in speech labs.
I think everyone can learn a language in his own country even if it is very
difficult and could really take a long time to gain good results.
15 In my opinion the grammar can be completely studied and memorized in your
own nation, but a decent and respectable speaking can only be obtained where
a language is used.

Comments

You should have ticked boxes **a**, **d**, **e**, **f**, **g** in Band 4, and boxes **b**, **c** in Band 5.

The answer is clear and accurate, with some very good structures, for example:
line 4 "nobody but a native speaker"
line 6/7 "not only ... but also"

There are some grammar mistakes, but these are minor:
line 2/3 "is living for several months" should be "is to live for several months"
line 11 "tapes listening" should be "listening to tapes"

There is some excellent vocabulary, for example:
line 9 "direct experience of a language"
line 14 "gain good results"

There are some mistakes in vocabulary:
line 12 "speech labs" should be "language labs"
line 16 "nation" should be "country"

The ideas expressed are clear and logical; they are in separate paragraphs, but the division could have been shown more clearly, at *lines 6, 11* and *15*.

Now read this sample answer to the same Exam Exercise, *use the marking key* and try to grade it. Then answer the questions, which focus on organisation of ideas and clarity. You will find comments and answers to the questions on page 64.

1 There are many ways to learn a foreign language, for example in evening classes, listening to cassettes at home or in the car, living in a country for a certain time or having a private teacher.
   In my opinion it depends on the individual person. The most important thing is
5 that the person wants to learn the language. The will and the readiness have to exist.
   I think the best and most successful way to learn a language is a stay in the country for a certain time, approximately for six months. I was in Britain to learn English and that is the reason why I have my own experience.
10 You are the whole day together with people who speak the language which you want to learn. Therefore you are forced to speak the language if you want to communicate with other people. All the other learning methods are not so intensive and effective, because you learn the language only for a certain time per day and you are not really forced to speak the language.
15 Besides, it needs much more time to learn the language that way.
   In conclusion I still want to say "If you want to learn a foreign language, you have to live in the language's country."

Questions

1 There are some mistakes:
   line 10 word order
   line 15 wrong verb
2 How can you improve the paragraphing and layout?

"SIX MONTHS OF CLASSES, THREE MONTHS OF LISTENING TO CASSETTES, AND I STILL CANT UNDERSTAND WHERE THE POST OFFICE IS"

If you would like to, you can study one of the five "set books", and then in Part 2 you can answer a question based on your reading of that book if you wish. On the exam paper the books are called Background Reading Texts.

Exam tip

> To do well at the set book question, you need to be good at reading comprehension and have a wide range of vocabulary. You must also be able to write clearly and concisely. This may be the reason why not many candidates answer this question. If you think you are at the level of a basic pass, it might be better not to attempt it. However, if you are above the basic level, we would recommend it, as it would give you the chance to show some originality.

BACKGROUND READING TEXTS

These are the set books at the time of writing this book.

Charles Dickens "Great Expectations" (Longman Bridge/Longman Fiction)
Daphne Du Maurier "Rebecca" (Longman Fiction)
Aldous Huxley "Brave New World" (Longman Bridge/Longman Fiction)
Oxford Bookworm Collections "Crime Never Pays" (OUP)
G. B. Shaw "Pygmalion" (any edition)

Note: Some of the books on the set book list change each year, so you should ask for an up-to-date list when you register for the exam.

Exam tip

> Remember, if you don't like the set book question when you take the exam, then don't answer it! If you *do* answer it, remember to put the number "5" in the box at the top of the page, and then write the title of the book next to it.

PREPARATION

The set book question is the same one for **all** five books, so you can't be asked anything specific to one book. You can expect to be asked general questions, though, such as:

- What makes the book exciting?
- Which is the most interesting character?
- How important is the title?
- How does the picture on the cover relate to the story?
- Is the ending of the book a satisfying one?
- Would you recommend the book you have read?

Note: All the work in this chapter, including the sample compositions and those in the Trial Papers, are based on "Great Expectations" and "Rebecca".

When reading any set book, you should make notes on:

- the main events in the story
- each of the main characters
- some short quotations connected to the events or characters that you could use to support the points you make in your composition.

NOTES ON *GREAT EXPECTATIONS*

Below is an example of how to make notes on a set book, based on "Great Expectations" by Charles Dickens.

a Main events

Pip, a little boy, meets Magwitch, an escaped prisoner, in a churchyard. Pip is kind to Magwitch and gives him food and drink. Later on, Pip goes to play with Estella, the adopted daughter of Miss Havisham, a strange rich lady. Mr. Jaggers, a lawyer, tells Pip that Pip has "great expectations", and can leave his job with the blacksmith to become a gentleman in London. Pip thinks that Miss Havisham is providing the money, but actually it has come from Magwitch, who became rich after leaving prison. Magwitch and Miss Havisham both die. Magwitch is revealed as Estella's father. Pip loves Estella, but it is not clear at the end of the book whether they will stay together.

b Character study: Pip

Pip is kind as a little boy, but becomes proud and selfish after becoming a gentleman, and he feels ashamed of his old friend Joe, the blacksmith. He is not grateful to Magwitch when he first discovers the truth about the money, and feels disgust as Magwitch is a criminal. Eventually he realises his mistakes and comes to a better understanding of himself. He learns to appreciate both Joe and Magwitch, and shows affection for them both, and concern for Magwitch's safety.

c Some short quotations

Mr. Jaggers: "Now, what I have to tell you is, that Pip has Great Expectations."

Magwitch: "You acted nobly, my boy, and I have never forgotten it."

Last line of book: "... in all the broad expanse of tranquil evening light, I saw no shadow of another parting."

NOTES ON *REBECCA*

Here is another example of how to make notes, based on "Rebecca" by Daphne du Maurier.

a Main events

Maxim de Winter, a widower, meets and marries a young woman who falls desperately in love with him. However, the spirit of his first wife, Rebecca, affects his second marriage to the young woman, who is telling the story. The newly married couple return to the family house, Manderley, where Rebecca had lived before with Maxim. Although Rebecca is dead, the housekeeper, Mrs. Danvers, will not accept the new wife and is determined to keep Rebecca's memory alive. This is made easier for her because Rebecca's body has never been found. The story follows the new bride as she slowly finds out more information about Rebecca, and the atmosphere becomes very threatening and strange. Maxim is accused of murder when Rebecca's body is discovered in a sunken boat, and although he had in fact committed this crime, he avoids discovery when the truth about Rebecca's fatal illness is revealed. The book ends when Manderley burns down.

b Character study: Mrs Danvers

She is described as having an evil and dangerous smile; her eyes and clothes are black, but her face is white. She hates the new Mrs. de Winter because she thinks that Rebecca was perfect and that no-one could ever take her place at Manderley. "She simply worshipped Rebecca". She does everything she can to make life difficult for the new bride, including telling her to wear the same dress that Rebecca had worn on the night she died, at the big fancy dress dance. She, like Rebecca, is an evil presence in the book, adding to the dangerous and threatening atmosphere.

c Some short quotations

Mrs Danvers:	"Sometimes I wonder if she comes back to Manderley and watches you and Mr. de Winter together."
About Mrs. de Winter:	"How different she is from Rebecca!"
First line of book:	"Last night I dreamed that I went to Manderley again."
About Rebecca:	"She was in the house still."
	"She knew she would win in the end."
	"She was the most beautiful creature I ever saw in my life."

EXAM EXERCISES

You have been invited to write a short article for your college magazine called *"The most exciting story I have ever read."*

SAMPLE COMPOSITION 1

Here is a sample answer to Exam Exercise 1. *Use the marking key* to try to grade it. Then read the comments under the answer to see if you were right.

1   This story is excellent and very thrilling.

  The murdered Rebecca, the first wife of Mr. Maxim de Winter, is the main character. Her spirit is everywhere and makes the life for her ex-husband and his second wife very difficult. From the moment the new couple comes to live

5   on the property Manderley, the past and its events covers their future plans with plenty of problems.

  From the moment an investigation is started concerning the found of a ship containing the dead body of Rebecca, the tension becomes unbearable! Maxim tells step by step his wife things about Rebecca and confesses frankly

10   he had killed her.

  The story from that point on becomes more and more exciting. Several questions like "Why did Maxim kill Rebecca?" "Who knows he did it?" "Will he be sent to prison?" involved me more and more in the action and the difficult situation of Maxim's second wife.

15   This story takes the reader out of the daily life and gives a feeling of being an onlooker, a bystander, in every new, dangerous, unpredictable situation.

  If you haven't read it yet ... it's worth to do so!

Comments

You should have ticked boxes **a, c, d, e, f, g** in Band 5, and box **b** in Band 4.

This is a good answer, which not only answers the question but is interesting to read. There is some interesting use of questions, direct speech and exclamation marks. The writer obviously knows the book well, and is able to give details from the story to make her points clear. It would have been an even better answer if she had actually quoted some words from the book itself, using speech marks (" "). However, she answers the question fully, and the conclusion is original and powerful.

There is a good variety of structure, such as:
> *line 4*   "From the moment the new couple ..."
> *line 11* "The story from that point on ..."

Although there are some grammatical mistakes, these are minor and do not affect understanding. They are:
> *line 7*   "the found" should be "the discovery"
> *line 17* "It's worth to do so" should be "It's worth doing so".

What makes this a good answer for the set book question is the way in which the writer has tried to use exciting vocabulary to show the excitement in the book; the composition is itself quite exciting to read. Some good use of vocabulary includes:
> *line 8*   "tension becomes unbearable"
> *line 15* "takes the reader out of daily life"
> *line 16* "dangerous, unpredictable situation"

The answer is well-organised in clear paragraphs, with a clear logical narrative which is easy to follow.

The style is exactly right, and the writer has also written imaginatively, using information at the beginning of the composition, "the murdered Rebecca", which actually comes from near the end of the book. This is clever as it shows the excitement in the book concisely and easily.

Now read this sample answer to the same Exam Exercise, *use the marking key* and try to grade it. Then answer the questions under the composition, which will focus on accuracy, and on content, style and presentation. You will find comments and answers to the questions on page 64.

SAMPLE COMPOSITION 2

1   What is the most exciting story I have read in my life? It is "Great
    Expectations"! The start is frightening when the prisoner is coming, "Keep still
    or I'll cut your throat!" We are wondering who he is, and what happen next.
    Then the visits to the strange lady, Miss Havisham and meeting
5   Mr. Jaggers continue the excitement. I thought the money was from Miss
    Havisham, but the evening Magwitch is coming to explain everything was
    a big shock. It was also exciting. What will happen to him? I also wanted to know
    how about Pip and Estella? I hope they will get marry, but the end is not so
    sure because in the book is "I saw no shadow of another parting".
10 Anyway, to my opinion, they are together. This is a good end to the exciting story!

Questions

1 How much detail does the writer give about the main characters in the novel?
2 How does the writer show that the book has an exciting start?
3 This composition should have had four paragraphs. Write the line numbers that should start the second, third and fourth paragraphs.
   paragraph 2 =
   paragraph 3 =
   paragraph 4 =
4 Find the mistakes in the following lines:
   line 2   wrong tense
   line 3   wrong tense
   line 5   "_____s"
   line 6   wrong tense
   line 8   unnecessary word / wrong form of the word
   line 10 wrong preposition

EXAM EXERCISE 2

Does the title of the book give a clear idea of what is involved in the story? Explain why you think it is or it is not a good title.

Here is a sample answer to Exam Exercise 2. *Use the marking key* and try to grade it. Then read the comments and see if you were right.

SAMPLE COMPOSITION 1

1   At first I did not understand why Charles Dickens gave this title to his novel
    but the title gradually became clear to me as I read the book.
    I think it is an excellent title because the central part of the story involves the
    metamorphosis in Pip's fortunes (Pip is the main character of "Great Expectations".)
5   With reference to this I want to quote why Mr. Jaggers, a lawyer in the novel,
    said about Pip "Now, what I have to tell you is that Pip has Great Expectations".
    Pip believes his expectations are connected with Miss Havisham (a strange
    rich lady) and for that reason he was very happy, but he was wrong.
    Magwitch, a person that he helped in the past and who became rich after
10 escaping from prison and going to Australia, had supplied the money that Pip
    invested to enable him leave his job with the blacksmith.
    Eventually Pip discovers the truth about the money and feels shock, as this was
    different from his expectations.
    So, the words "Great Expectations" are a kind of summary of the story.

Comments

You should have ticked boxes **b**, **d**, **e**, **f**, **g** in Band 5, and boxes **a**, **c** in Band 4.

This is basically a good answer; the writer has answered the question, although he does not give much detail about the narrative. The use of quotation is good, but he could have said more about what the expectations actually were and how they changed Pip's life.

The grammatical structures are accurate, although there are some minor mistakes in vocabulary; the use of "metamorphosis" in *line 4* is a good example of how a word in one language can transfer in meaning to English but is not an appropriate style. It would have been better to use the word "change".

The word "shock" in *line 12* is also not appropriate – it would have been better to use it as a verb, and say "he was shocked".

The presentation of ideas is good, with a good introduction which sets out the answer clearly, and the conclusion is logical and confirms the points made in the answer. The layout would have been better if the writer had left a line between the paragraphs as he has used block style, to make the paragraphs clear.

The style is exactly right for this kind of writing.

SAMPLE COMPOSITION 2

Now read the following answer to the same Exam Exercise. *Use the marking key* and try to grade it. Then answer the questions under the composition, which will focus on accuracy, content and style. You will find comments and answers to the questions on page 65.

1 This title gives at first a wrong impression of the book. Before opening it, when you read "Rebecca", you think it a love story. But, as soon as you enter in the book, you start to understand the title and think it's a good one. And finally, when you close it, you can't even think to another one: This short title
5 gives the idea of the overpresence of Rebecca at Manderley and involves the complex personality of this woman.

Rebecca is actually dead. She was the first wife of Max de Winter and seemed to be the "perfect wife" for the new Mrs de Winter and for anybody else. Her shadow is still so present that she seems still alive. She's a real spirit haunting
10 Manderley.

However, this title is very well chosen because Rebecca means at the same time everything and nothing at all. We know only her name. And what is a name? Does it reveal someone's character? No, that gives only the illusion we know her.

15 For those reasons, I think the title of this book is very well chosen.

Questions

1 Does this composition give you a clear idea of Rebecca's part in the book?
2 Which sentence describes Rebecca's presence very well?
3 Would this composition make you want to read the book?
4 Find the mistakes in the following lines:

line 2 missing verb
line 3 unnecessary preposition
line 4 wrong preposition
line 5 wrong word

EXAM
EXERCISE 3

A teacher you know has asked you to recommend one of the set books on the list for her class to study next term. Describe the main points of the story of the book you have read, and say why the class might find it interesting.

SAMPLE
COMPOSITION 1

Here is a sample answer to Exam Exercise 3. It relates to "Great Expectations". *Use the marking key* and try to grade it, then read the comments and answer the questions, which focus on content and vocabulary. You will find answers to the questions on page 65.

1   I would recommend "Great Expectations" because it is a fascinating novel with many unexpected turns of events that will leave a lasting impression on the reader.
It is the story of an orphan boy named Pip who helps an escaped prisoner, Magwitch, by stealing food. Determined to leave this incident behind him, he signs an apprenticeship with Joe, the
5   blacksmith, with the expectation of one day being other than a common labourer boy for the sake of Estella, whom he loves. This great expectation comes true and Pip is taken to London (on the condition that he must not learn the name of his benefactor) to be brought up as a gentleman. There he meets Estella again and finds that he still loves her even though she confides in him that she is only after breaking men's hearts to revenge Miss Havisham, whose life was shattered when
10   she was jilted on her wedding day. Now is the time for Magwitch the ex-convict returns to reveal how he has repayed Pip for the kindness he showed him years earlier. Pip is destroyed to find where his money has come from until he learns that Magwitch is Estella's father and all their lives take a whole new turn ...

Comments

This is clearly a Band 5 composition, with a very wide range of structures and vocabulary. (The only mistakes are "destroyed" in *line 11*, which should be "distraught", and "repayed" in *line 11*, which should be spelt "repaid".)

Questions

1 The composition gives a full account of the story. Note down five different events in the book that you have learned from reading this composition.

2 The use of vocabulary in the composition is very effective. Note down how the writer describes what happened to Miss Havisham and how the characters' lives change.

SAMPLE
COMPOSITION 2

Now read this sample answer to the same Exam Exercise. It relates to "Rebecca". *Use the marking key* and try to grade it. Then answer the questions under the composition, which also focus on content and vocabulary. You will find comments and answers to the questions on page 65.

1   I personally recommend "Rebecca" by Daphne du Maurier because I thought this book was really exciting. It is both full of suspense and emotion. Through the new Mrs. De Winter, the narrator, we discover the life of a young married couple whose life is haunted by the ghost of Rebecca, the first wife of Mr. de Winter.
5   The book starts by the come-back of the narrator at Manderley in her dreams. She describes it as the "lost paradise" and we therefore wonder, and also throughout the story, what could have happened to the place. We have the clue only in the last five lines of the book, that Manderley has been blown up on fire. The atmosphere is always very strained because of the presence of Rebecca, who, although dead, ruins the couple's life. The narrator always compares herself to the image she
10 has of Rebecca. Even when Mrs. De Winter has at last learnt the truth about Rebecca's bad side, and she is not mixed up any more, Rebecca wins because Manderley is set on fire.

Questions

1 Note down any events in the book that are described in this composition.

2 Note down the expression used to describe the effect Rebecca has on the life of the young couple, and the word that describes the atmosphere in the house.

3 Find the mistakes in the following lines:
line 5 wrong preposition/wrong word
line 8 wrong verb

Trial Paper A

PART 1

You **must** answer this question.

1   Your family is interested in hiring the car shown in the "Funcars" brochure, but needs more information. You have the task of writing to the manager of "Funcars", who published the advertisement.

Read carefully the advertisement and the notes which you have made below. Then write your letter to "Funcars", covering the points in your notes and adding any relevant information about your family.

Write a **letter** of between **120** and **180** words in an appropriate style. Do not write any addresses.

FUNCARS

✦   *Carefree motoring.*
✦   *No hidden extras.*
✦   *Low prices for weekly rental.*
✦   *Valid driving licence required.*

- need a luggage rack. Is this an "extra"?

- price for two weeks?

- can we collect car at airport?

- pay in travellers' cheques?

- one driver under 21. Is this all right?

- is international driving licence acceptable?

(There is a model answer on page 65.)

PART 2

Write an answer to **one** of the questions **2-5** in this part. Write your answer in **120-180** words in an appropriate style.

2   You have recently started work for a company that publishes a guide to hotels. You have visited the "Seaview Hotel", and must now write a report for your boss, Mr. Anderson.

Write your **report** describing the hotel, what it has to offer to tourists and commenting on its good and bad points.

3   Your teacher has asked you to write a story beginning with these words:

"*The day trip to the beach started badly.*"

Write the **story**.

4   Your English penfriend has asked you to send him/her information about places of interest in your city for a project on "*Places around the world*".

Write the **letter**, giving information about your *two* favourite places, giving reasons for your choice.

5   **Background reading texts**

Answer the following question based on your reading of **one** of these books.

Great Expectations by Charles Dickens (Longman Bridge/Longman Fiction)
Rebecca by Daphne Du Maurier (Longman Fiction)
Brave New World by Aldous Huxley (Longman Bridge/Longman Fiction)
Crime Never Pays, Oxford Bookworm Collections (OUP)
Pygmalion by G. B. Shaw (any edition)

Novels have either happy or sad endings, or are rather "open-ended". Describe the ending of the book you have read, and say if it is a good way of ending the story.

(**Note:** you can write on any of these books, but the model answers will come from "Great Expectations" and "Rebecca".)

(There are model answers on pages 66-67.)

Trial Paper B

PART 1

You **must** answer this question.

1   Your family is interested in the skiing holiday in the "Ski-Days" brochure, but needs more information. You have the task of writing to the manage of "Ski-Days", Mrs J. Thompson, who published the brochure.

   Read carefully the brochure and the notes which you have made below. Then write your letter to "Ski-Days", covering the points in your notes and adding any relevant information about your family.

   Write a **letter** of between **120** and **180** words in an appropriate style. Do not write any addresses.

Only 5 kms from ski-slopes ✦ Delicious local meals
Hire of skis and boots available ✦ Evening activities
"Gold Medal" races on last day

- are the meals included?
- price of skis and boots? Pay in advance?
- what exactly are the evening activities?
- more details of races
- how do we get to ski-slopes?
- no details of cost of ski-lift

(There is a model answer on page 67.)

PART 2

Write an answer to **one** of the questions **2-5** in this part. Write your answer in **120-180** words in an appropriate style.

2   An international young person's magazine is investigating the question:

   Should young people spend a year working in the local community after leaving school?

   Write an **article** for this magazine on this topic, based on your own experience.

3   You have decided to enter a short-story competition. The competition rules say that the story must begin or end with the following words:

   "*As John walked sadly away, a tear slowly trickled down his face.*"

   Write your **story** for the competition.

4

> ## SOCIAL ACTIVITIES OFFICER
>
> Student required to organise excursions and some sports for our foreign language students.
>
> *Good at organisation?*
>
> *Like visiting historic cities?*
>
> *Sporty?*
>
> *Speak another language?*
>
> To apply, write us a letter saying what makes you suitable for this job.

   Write your **letter** of application to the Principal. Do not write any addresses.

5   **Background reading texts**

   Answer the following question based on your reading of **one** of these set books.

   Great Expectations by Charles Dickens (Longman Bridge/Longman Fiction)
   Rebecca by Daphne Du Maurier (Longman Fiction)
   Brave New World by Aldous Huxley (Longman Bridge/Longman Fiction)
   Crime Never Pays, Oxford Bookworm Collections (OUP)
   Pygmalion by G. B. Shaw (any edition)

   Describe a character in the story you've read and say why he or she is important.

   (**Note:** you can write on any of these books, but the model answers will come from "Great Expectations" and "Rebecca").

(There are model answers on pages 68-69.)

Answers and Notes

1 INTRODUCTION

2 noun
3 verb
4 adverb
5 preposition
6 pronoun

PRACTICE EXERCISE

My friend, John, works in a bank. John and his colleague, Michael, have only been there for three months, but they are happy there. John is going to get married to Michael's sister, Lucy, next month. They haven't bought a new house yet. Last Saturday they spent all day looking at houses, but couldn't find one they liked. They might have to live in the flat John bought last year. John likes his flat, but Lucy doesn't!

2 PART 1: COMPULSORY QUESTION

PRACTICE EXERCISE 1

1 we're
2 There/Their
3 It's
4 whose
5 its
6 how
7 here
8 whether
9 wear
10 hear
11 right
12 Though
13 whole

PRACTICE EXERCISE 2

1 practise
2 learning
3 bring
4 advise
5 opportunity
6 receipt

PRACTICE EXERCISE 3

a 3, b 4, c 1, d 2

PRACTICE EXERCISE 4

With reference to your letter which I received yesterday
I would like to confirm that the price is satisfactory
I would appreciate your help
I look forward to hearing from you
Yours sincerely

Here is an improved version of the composition.

Dear Susan,

Thank you for your letter, which came yesterday. I hope you are enjoying your stay here.

I would like to meet you on Wednesday morning: any time after 10 o'clock would be fine. Could you please ring me on 48572 to confirm the time?

I am interested in hearing about your research into marriage customs, and also winter festivals such as Christmas, which is very important for us. I would also like to see any photographs that you have taken, and would like to take a photograph of you for our magazine.

Finally, my readers would be interested in finding out why you have come to this country.

I'm looking forward to meeting you next week; my friend will not be coming with me after all, but he sends his regards.

With best wishes,

John

You should have ticked boxes **b**, **c**, **d**, **e**, **g** in Band 3, and boxes **a**, **f** in Band 2, as the writer has missed the information about the bridge, and has made a mistake in the style of the ending.

1 yes – the bridge
2 no – the letter should end like the first answer to this question
3 yes – reasons for bringing the dog; question about karaoke
4 *line 3*   "watched" should be "saw"
      line 13   I look forward to hearing from you soon.

You should have ticked boxes **a**, **b**, **c**, **e**, **f**, **g** in Band 4 and box **d** in Band 3.

1 There are too many paragraphs, and they do not relate to new ideas.
2 "In fact, I saw the advertisement for the College in the local newspaper and I'm interested in taking a French course. Although I studied French some years ago, I haven't been able to practise it since then, and I've forgotten almost everything."
3 *line 9/10* "I'd like some information from you that I couldn't find in the ad."
      line 15   "You seem to have a great time" should be "You seem to be having a great time"
      line 17   earlier

3 PART 2: REPORTS AND ARTICLES

1 although
2 Despite
3 because
4 but
5 However

However   Secondly   In addition to this   Finally

c, a, d, b

PRACTICE EXERCISE 4

Report

For: Committee chairman

On: Festival planning meeting

It was suggested that the festival should take place over a three-day period, probably from Friday to Sunday at the end of July.

Regarding the location for the festival, most people thought that Central Park would be the most convenient place. The nearby church would provide plenty of parking space for visitors to the festival.

There was a discussion concerning what to do with the money raised by the festival, and it was generally agreed that some local charities should benefit from it – for example, the local cancer research unit.

There seems to be general agreement that the festival is a good idea, especially since it will bring a great deal of business into the town, benefiting local shops, restaurants and hotels.

Therefore I feel that we should support the proposal for a festival in Central Park at the end of July.

EXAM EXERCISE 1

SAMPLE COMPOSITION 2

You should have ticked boxes **b**, **d**, **g** in Band 3, and **a**, **c**, **e**, **f** in Band 4

1 *lines 1-4* arrived/changed (instead of "would arrive" and "would be changed")
   line 10 the heart

   Note: it would have been better to put "why" instead of "because of which" in *line 14*.

2 There should have been a clearer indication of where the new paragraphs start (*lines 5, 10* and *14*.)

EXAM EXERCISE 2

SAMPLE COMPOSITION 2

You should have ticked boxes **a**, **c**, **d**, **f** in Band 4 and **b**, **e**, **g** in Band 3.

line 1 it / beautifully
line 3 it
line 4 with (before "intimate")
line 6 it
line 7 However (instead of "But") / it (before "is")
line 8 which (instead of "where")
line 10 eating (instead of "to eat")
line 11 it
line 13 that the restaurant has

Note: The writer makes the same mistake in *lines 1, 3, 6* and *11*. You cannot put "it" if there is a subject word already.

PRACTICE EXERCISE 5

e, a, d, c, b, f
1 delay
2 the scene

PRACTICE EXERCISE 6

The man ran out of the big house, carrying a bag. **It** was heavy, and **he** couldn't run very fast. Suddenly, two policemen appeared around the corner and saw **him**. **They** shouted at **him**, and started to run after **him**. The man dropped the bag, and one of the policemen picked **it** up. **He** opened **it**, and saw that **it** was full of books. **They** were very valuable, and **they** had been stolen from the house.

This text is more interesting than the first one, because you do not need to repeat the same words all the time.

There was a meeting held last night to discuss the plans for a festival to be held in the town. It soon became clear that the majority of residents were against the plan, for a variety of reasons. Most people felt that the period of three days was too long, and the proposed site of Central Park was not popular as people who live near the Park were afraid of being disturbed by too much noise. The suggestion of using the church for parking was rejected, because people felt that there was not enough room there, and that parking was already difficult enough in the town without causing more problems. The disadvantage of having too many tourists in the town seemed to be greater than the advantage of the extra business the tourists would bring. Clearly, local residents were also worried about the large number of people that would crowd into the town while the festival was taking place.

Report: 1a 2d 3e 4g   **Article:** 1b 2c 3f

Living in a town is very exciting, because there is so much to do there. There are many different sports facilities, so there's always some activity to take part in, and there are different types of clubs to join if you want to. These clubs are good places to meet people and make new friends. Furthermore, you can find a variety of shops where you can buy anything you want. Finally, the bus services are usually good, so there's no problem getting about at any time.

Omit 2 + 6   because they are irrelevant
Omit 3 + 9   because they are disadvantages

Omit 1 + 4   as these are not problems
Omit 6   because this is not *caused by* smoking

The main problem caused by smoking is that it can cause lung cancer, which kills thousands of people every year. The smoke can also cause secondary cancer in other people in the room, and can irritate non-smokers trying to enjoy a meal in a restaurant. Further problems can be caused by fires started by cigarette ends being dropped when they are still alight.

You should have ticked all the boxes in Band 4.
line 1   the (before "people")
line 4   was (instead of "has been")
line 6   "propaganda" usually relates to politics; the word here should be "programmes"
line 8   about ("we read about a terrible happening")

You should have ticked boxes **b**, **c**, **e**, **f**, **g** in Band 3 and **a**, **d** in Band 2.

This is not a well-planned composition, as it is really just a list of places the writer would like to go to.

Improved composition

When I thought about my ideal holiday, I thought about where I would like to visit, but I couldn't choose one particular place because I wanted to go round the world.

If I went round the world, I would start in the Far East, in China, so that I could see the Great Wall and walk a little way along it. After that, I would move on to Thailand so that I could lie on the beach there.

Then I would visit India and Africa; the former, because I want to see the River Ganges, where people purify their spirits and souls, and the latter because I'd like to see wild animals such as lions, panthers and elephants.

Finally, after shopping in Europe, I would finish my journey in the United States, because I want to listen to all the different kinds of music there, from Jazz and Rhythm and Blues, to Rock 'n' Roll. That would make me very happy.

If I went round the world, I could grow up. I would see people, scenes, places and hear other languages and music that would change me for ever. I would love to do that, and that is the reason that it would be my ideal holiday.

4 PART 2: WRITING A STORY

PRACTICE EXERCISE 1

b, d, f, c, e, a, g

PRACTICE EXERCISE 2

1 exciting
2 carelessly
3 terrifying
4 silently
5 threateningly
6 depressing
7 thrilling
8 deafening

PRACTICE EXERCISE 3

Ways of walking
1 crept
2 limped
3 marched
4 rushed

Ways of looking
1 glancing
2 watching
3 staring
4 frowned

Ways of speaking
1 screamed
2 whispering
3 shouted
4 called

PRACTICE EXERCISE 4

wonderful time
comfortable bus
friendly driver
funny stories
luxurious room
delicious food
soft music

EXAM EXERCISE 1

SAMPLE COMPOSITION 2

You should have ticked boxes **a**, **c**, **d**, **e**, **f**, **g** in Band 4 and box **b** in Band 3.
line 5   it
line 8   "with" should be "by"
line 9   in
line 11 went (instead of "had gone") / turned (instead of "had turned")
line 12 corrected (instead of "had corrected") / went (instead of "had gone")
line 14 met (instead of "had met") / was (instead of "had been")
line 15 asked (instead of "had asked")
line 16 answered (instead of "had answered")
line 17 they have been killed.
line 18 went (instead of "had gone") / closed (instead of "had closed")
Note: The writer does not understand that the Past Perfect tense "had done" indicates an action before the one in the Past Simple "did". You should use the Past Simple tense for the main actions in the past in your story.

You should have ticked boxes **a**, **d** in Band 4 and **b**, **c**, **e**, **f**, **g** in Band 3.

line 1 before I tell you
line 7 about (before "the wedding day")
line 8 her (before "away")
line 10 passing slowly (instead of "spending slow")
line 13 fell asleep (instead of "was falling asleep") / woke (instead of "waked")

Improved composition

"What a boring holiday!" Susan thought to herself. It had been wonderful at first, but the rest of the time had been horrible, with problems at the hotel and arguments over a restaurant bill. To make matter worse, she had spent nearly all her money.

She had met a nice young boy called Tom quite early on. Although they liked each other, they were too shy to say very much. On her final day, she decided to have a last swim before lunch. When she had finished swimming, she went to a restaurant alone to have lunch. Afterwards, she returned to the beach, but she had eaten a lot so she wanted to have a siesta. She lay on the sand for some time, and then went swimming. Because she was so full, she started to drown.

Tom saw her, and rescued her. When Susan opened her eyes, she saw him standing over her. This was the start of their new relationship. Susan gazed into his eyes, and she could hardly believe that her dream had come true with the man who had always loved her and never given up hope.

You should have ticked boxes **a**, **c**, **d**, **g** in Band 3, and boxes **b**, **e**, **f** in Band 4.

1 *line 2* "I was so surprised"
 line 11 "so shocked"
2 *line 4/5* Trembling with fear, I went slowly from room to room, checking what the robber had stolen. (6 extra words)
 line 9 For the next few days I couldn't stop thinking about this, and kept imagining that the robber would return. (19 extra words)

5 PART 2: WRITING A LETTER

1 Dear Jane,

I am writing to thank you for the great party last week. It was really enjoyable, and it was nice to see all my old friends again.

I'm looking forward to seeing you again next month at the school reunion. Could you please bring some things for me that I can't find here? I'd like some tea, coffee and an English grammar book.

By the way, I met John last week and he asked me to say "Hi!" to you.

With thanks and best wishes,

Mary

2 Dear Sue,

Guess who I saw last week – James! He'd been to visit Jane's friend Peter, and I bumped into him quite by chance in the pub. He was really well, and told me to say "Hi" to you. He's going to France next week to start a new job there, so I suppose we won't see him for some time.

I just thought you would be interested.

See you soon,

Love,

Andrew

PRACTICE EXERCISE 2

Formal: b, c, f, h, d, k
Informal: a, e, i, j, g, l

EXAM EXERCISE 1

SAMPLE COMPOSITION 2

You should have ticked boxes **a**, **c**, **e**, **g** in Band 4, and boxes **b**, **d**, **f** in Band 3.
1 *line 7* I have been working there for the last twenty years.
line 12 feel that they are having a good time but are also learning something about the past.
line 15 are now grown-ups
2 The sentences in the wrong style are: "Like answering different questions? Yes ..."
The letter should begin "Dear Sir" and end "Yours faithfully".

EXAM EXERCISE 2

SAMPLE COMPOSITION 2

You should have ticked boxes **b**, **c**, **e**, **g** in Band 3 and boxes **a**, **d**, **f** in Band 4.
    The mistakes in structure and vocabulary prevent a higher mark, and have a less positive effect on the reader.
1 *"It starts by talking about the good and bad points at each stage of life, from the teenage years to old age. The interesting thing is that not only does it discuss a serious subject like the responsibilities that come with being an adult, but it also shows you the way to start this new stage of life by making the best choices."*
2 *line 16* do (after "I")

EXAM EXERCISE 3

SAMPLE COMPOSITION 2

You should have ticked boxes **a**, **f**, **g** in Band 5 and boxes **b**, **c**, **d**, **e** in Band 4.
1 The second, because it gives detail and feelings.
2 Newspapers, reports, vocabulary, grammar test, video.
3 The test was difficult / we enjoyed making a video
4 *line 4* to (before "a dialogue") / the (before "telephone")
line 9 the (before "last week")
line 10 did a test / the (before "passive")
line 11 speak about it
line 13 We made a video by ourselves!

EXAM EXERCISE 4

SAMPLE COMPOSITION 2

You should have ticked all the boxes in Band 4.
1 *line 10* "You are together with people who speak the language you want to learn, the whole day."
line 15 "Besides, it takes much more time to learn the language"
2 The division between the paragraphs could be made clearer. They should start at *lines 4*, *7*, and *16*.

6 PART 2: SET BOOK

EXAM EXERCISE 1

SAMPLE COMPOSITION 2

You should have ticked all the boxes in Band 3.
1 The writer assumes that the reader already knows the main characters: he hasn't really described them.
2 By giving the direct quotation "Keep still ..."
3 paragraph 2 = *line 4*
paragraph 3 = *line 7* ("I also wanted to know ...")
paragraph 4 = *line 10*
4 *line 2* comes (instead of "is coming")
line 3 wonder (instead of "are wondering")
line 5 continues
line 6 comes (instead of "is coming")
line 8 how / married (instead of "marry")
line 10 it should be "in my opinion"

Note: The mistake in *lines 2*, *3* and *6* is the same; the continuous form has been used instead of the simple form.

You should have ticked boxes **a**, **d**, **e**, **f**, **g** in Band 5, and **b**, **c** in Band 4.

1 Yes, it points out that she seems to be alive even though she is dead.

2 "She's a real spirit haunting Manderley".

3 Probably, because it makes you wonder what effect Rebecca's spirit will have.

4 *line 2*   it is a love story
   line 3   in
   line 4   think of
   line 5   overpresence (it should be "presence" or "omnipresence")

EXAM
EXERCISE 2

SAMPLE
COMPOSITION 2

1 Pip helps an escaped prisoner by stealing food.
   Pip signs an apprenticeship with Joe, the blacksmith.
   Pip is taken to London to be brought up as a gentleman.
   Pip meets Estella again and realises he still loves her.
   Magwitch returns to reveal the truth to Pip.

2 Her life was shattered when she was jilted on her wedding day.

EXAM
EXERCISE 3

SAMPLE
COMPOSITION 1

You should have ticked boxes **a**, **d**, **f**, **g** in Band 5, and **b**, **c**, **e** in Band 4.

1 The only real event that is described is the fire at Manderley. (However, the composition gives a very good feeling of how exciting the book is, by concentrating on the atmosphere).

2 "haunted by the ghost of Rebecca"
   "strained"

3 *line 5*   with (instead of "by") / the return (instead of "come-back")
   line 8   set (instead of "blown up")

SAMPLE
COMPOSITION 2

TRIAL PAPER A

There are **no** mistakes in these compositions, and they would **all** be placed in Band 5.

MODEL
ANSWERS

PART 1

1 Dear Sir,

   I am interested in hiring a medium-sized car, as advertised in your brochure.

   Could you please let me know the cost for two weeks in August? I would prefer to pay in travellers' cheques, if this is possible.

   Your brochure states that a valid driving licence is required, but does an international driving licence count as valid? I would also like to know if your insurance will cover my brother, who has a full licence but is under 21 years old.

   I understand that you have "no hidden extras", but my family will require a luggage rack, and I wonder if that could also be included in the basic cost.

   Finally, we would prefer to pick the car up at the airport rather than come to the city centre, so could you please confirm that this will be possible.

   Thanking you for your attention in this matter,

   Yours faithfully,

   F. Smith

2 Report

For: J. Anderson

From: M. Smith

Date: 5th July

Subject: Seaview Hotel, Devonshire

I visited the above hotel last weekend, and I am now sending the report you requested.

Firstly, the Seaview Hotel, as the name suggests, overlooks the sea, and provides a magnificent view of the beach from all the rooms, and also from the splendid seafood restaurant on the top floor. All the bedrooms are equipped to a high standard, but I am afraid that some of the bathrooms leave a lot to be desired. However, this matter is being dealt with and should cause no problems in the future.

The service in all parts of the hotel is satisfactory, and the special price for an extended weekend for two people is amazingly low.

In addition to all this, the local town is only 5 minutes' walk away, providing guests with an excellent shopping centre where lots of bargains can be found.

If you could come to my office on Tuesday afternoon, I could give you further details and show you the hotel brochure.

3   The day trip to the beach started badly. I realised this as soon as I woke up and found that we had all overslept by two hours. Then, rushing to the motorway which leads to the coast, we were shocked when one of our front tyres blew up, and we had to wait nearly two hours for help.

    Once we arrived at the beach, we hired a motorboat and started to "ride the waves". Believe it or not, we ran out of petrol and had to be towed back to the harbour!

    Just as we were about to give up and go home, we noticed a group of boys playing football with an older man. Suddenly we realised who it was – Pele, the most famous footballer in the world! We joined in the game, and I even ran past Pele to score a goal.

    We went home talking excitedly about our great match, and the troubles of the morning were all forgotten.

4 Dear Peter,

    It was great to hear from you again, and get up-to-date with all your news. I'm so glad to hear you're doing so well at college.

    You asked me about places of interest in my city, Milan. Well, I've got two favourite places, the cathedral and the theatre. Our cathedral is full of history, and every time I go there I seem to travel back in time! The architecture is magnificent, and the stained glass windows are really amazing.

    Our theatre, "La Scala", is well-known all over the world (even in England, I think!) and last week we were lucky enough to see the great Pavarotti. His voice is almost unbelievable, but unfortunately the prices were, too!

    Of course, there's a lot more to see and do in Milan, and don't forget our fashion industry is now almost as famous as Paris.

    Anyway, I hope you can use this information in your project. Give me a ring if you want any more information.

    Hoping to see you soon,

    Best wishes,

    Giovanna.

5   <u>Great Expextations</u>

Charles Dickens' "Great Expectations" presents an open ending, as the reader finishes it without knowing whether Estella and Pip stay together or not.

On the one hand, the last sentence of the book – "I saw no shadow of another parting" – can mean that there will be an inevitable parting (although Pip is unable to see it at the moment), either because the truth is unbearable or because he believes that Estella is not serious about it.

On the other hand, there is another way of interpreting this final sentence. Instead of understanding that the couple will be apart, the reader may infer that Pip's reason for not seeing the "shadow of another parting" is that he is absolutely certain that Estella will not leave him again.

I think that Dickens' ambiguous end is a good way of concluding the story, mainly because it gives the reader – and not the writer, as usually happens – an opportunity to choose the end they consider most suitable.

5   <u>Rebecca</u>

The ending of "Rebecca" is essentially a sad one, as we discover that Manderley has burned down and "the ashes blew towards us with the salt wind from the sea".

In a way, the ending shows us that the spirit of the dead Rebecca is triumphant, and the new Mrs. de Winter has not been able to prevent her influence on the lives of everyone at Manderley.

Throughout her married life, the new Mrs. De Winter has to fight against the hatred of Rebecca's housekeeper, Mrs. Danvers, who ultimately gets a kind of revenge by setting Manderley on fire.

The opening sentence of the book shows us that the new Mrs. de Winter still dreams of Manderley and perhaps has nightmares about the ashes of the great house. Perhaps she will never find peace of mind again.

TRIAL PAPER B

There are **no** mistakes in these compositions, and they would **all** be placed in Band 5.

MODEL ANSWERS

PART 1

1   Dear Mrs. Thompson,

Thank you for sending me the "Ski-Days" brochure, which I received yesterday.

Before making a definite reservation, I would like to ask for some further information.

Firstly, I am not sure how we would get from the hotel to the ski slopes, especially as they are 5 kilometres away.

Secondly, I cannot find any mention of the cost of hiring skis and boots, and the use of the ski lifts. (We would like to pay for all this in advance if possible.)

My other questions concern meals and activities. I would like to know if the meals are included in the basic cost of the holiday, and could you let me have more details about what happens in the evenings. My family is particularly interested in this, and would also like to know about the "Gold Medal" races, which sound very exciting.

I would be grateful if you could reply to these points as soon as possible.

Yours sincerely,

M. Jones

2 I am in two minds about this question, since the idea of young people working in the local community has pros and cons.

It might appear to be a very good idea to encourage young people to think of others and do something to help the elderly, or people who are disadvantaged in some way. Many young people are rather selfish, and the experience would benefit them as much as the people they would be helping.

However, on further consideration, it does not seem right to force young people to do something against their will.

It may be better to let young people continue their education and obtain more experience of life, and then try to encourage some part-time help from people in their twenties. They would have more to offer, and their contribution would be more valuable because it would be voluntary.

On balance, therefore, I do not think that school leavers should spend a year working in the community.

3 As John walked sadly away, a tear slowly trickled down his face. It was the first time in his life that he had had to deal with anything unpleasant. He could hardly believe his ears. His parents' words kept repeating in his mind, "Sorry, son, we've got to move to another town."

How could they have taken such an important decision without consulting him? How could he leave all his friends and run away as if he had done something wrong? He couldn't understand this decision at all. This sort of situation is very difficult for teenagers to deal with.

In a week's time, they would all have to pack their belongings and try to settle down a long way from "home". It might be easy for his parents, but John would have to get used to a new school, different teachers and different classes, as well as trying to make new friends.

Although the future looked so uncertain, John was not aware that good news would soon be coming ...

4 Dear Sir,

I would like to apply for the position of Social Activities Officer as advertised in "The Times" yesterday.

I am at present working as an assistant social organiser for the Tower School in London, and I am responsible for organising school trips to all the places of interest in London.

In the afternoons, my duties involve running the sports course, which is part of our "Special Subjects" programme, and I give extra sports coaching for tennis and football on Sunday afternoons.

I really enjoy working with young people from all over the world, and this gives me the chance to practise my French, Italian and German, my main foreign languages.

I feel that my experience in organising trips, my involvement in the sports programme and my knowledge of languages all make me a suitable candidate for the job.

I would be delighted to attend an interview at any time, and look forward to hearing from you.

Yours sincerely

T. Mull

5 Rebecca

There are several strong characters in the story of "Rebecca", and even the house seems to have a character of its own, but I have chosen to talk about the new Mrs. de Winter.

We never find out her first name, so that she is a very quiet and colourless character in comparison with the beautiful and dangerous Rebecca. "How different she is from Rebecca!" However, she is very important as she is the narrator, so we see all the other characters through her eyes.

She meets Maxim in France, and can't believe her good luck when he falls in love with her. She is easily frightened, and living at Manderley with the evil housekeeper who hates her is very difficult. All she wants to do is to please Max and make him happy. However, she gains confidence, and as Max is drawn into the difficult and dramatic situation at the end of the book, he relies on his new wife more and more.

She is vital to the book, because without her the mystery of Rebecca would never have been solved. By coming to Manderley, she causes all the other events to happen.

5 Great Expectations

Magwitch is the character I have chosen. He makes a dramatic entrance at the start of the novel, when he grabs Pip in the churchyard. Dickens describes him as being "a fearful man, all in coarse grey, with a great iron on his leg".

After this, we do not hear of him again until Pip's "great expectations" are revealed. When Magwitch returns, he has become stronger and is tanned from exposure to the weather. His importance to the story then becomes crystal clear, as it was he who had provided the wealth for Pip and not Miss Havisham, as had been thought.

Pip had made a great impression on Magwitch in the churchyard, and that is why Magwitch resolved to make "a gentleman of him" if he could. The central part of the novel concerns Pip's changes in fortune from a blacksmith's apprentice to a prosperous young gentleman who might have the chance of winning Estella's love.

All this is achieved thanks to Magwitch's success in Australia. As he told Pip, "I've done wonderfully well".

As can be seen, therefore, Magwitch plays a vitally important role in the book.

MARKING KEY

Band 5

The composition: ✓

a answers the question fully, and with some original points	
b uses a wide range of grammatical structures correctly	
c uses a wide range of vocabulary correctly	
d has the ideas clearly organised in paragraphs	
e uses a variety of connecting words	
f is written in exactly the right style for this type of writing	
g has a very positive effect on the reader	

Band 4

The composition:

a answers the question with enough detail	
b uses a good range of grammatical structures, mostly correctly	
c uses a good range of vocabulary, mostly correctly	
d has the ideas organised in paragraphs	
e uses suitable connecting words	
f is in the right style for this type of writing	
g has a positive effect on the reader	

Band 3

The composition:

a answers the question	
b uses a satisfactory range of grammatical structures, with some errors	
c uses a satisfactory range of vocabulary	
d has the ideas basically organised in paragraphs	
e uses simple connecting words	
f is mostly in the right style for this type of writing	
g has a satisfactory effect on the reader	

Band 2

The composition:

a fails to answer the question fully, and/or is not always relevant	
b uses a limited range of grammatical structures, with errors which make communication difficult	
c uses a limited range of vocabulary with errors which make communication difficult	·
d does not have the ideas organised in paragraphs	
e uses few connecting words	
f is not in a style which is suitable for this type of writing	
g does not communicate clearly to the reader	

Band 1

The composition:

a leaves out some parts of the question, and/or has a lot of irrelevant points	
b uses a narrow range of grammatical structures, with many errors	
c uses a narrow range of vocabulary, with many errors	
d has no organisation of the ideas	
e uses no connecting words	
f shows no understanding of the style needed for this type of writing	
g has a very negative effect on the reader	